The Formal Theory of Grammar

PRENTICE-HALL FOUNDATIONS OF MODERN LINGUISTICS SERIES

Sanford A. Schane

editor

John P. Kimball The Formal Theory of Grammar
Robert P. Stockwell Foundations of Syntactic Theory
Sanford A. Schane Generative Phonology
Theo Vennemann Introduction to Historical Linguistics
Maurice Gross Mathematical Models in Linguistics
William S-Y. Wang Phonetics
Janet Dean Fodor Semantics
Suzette Haden Elgin What Is Linguistics?
Other titles to be announced

The Formal Theory of Grammar

JOHN P. KIMBALL

University of California, Santa Cruz

PRENTICE-HALL, INC., ENGLEWOOD CLIFFS, NEW JERSEY

Library of Congress Cataloging in Publication Data

KIMBALL, JOHN P
   The formal theory of grammar.

   (Foundations of modern linguistics)
   Bibliography: p. 127
   1. Grammar, Comparative and general. 2. Generative
grammar. 3. Semantics. I. Title.
P151.K55 1973   415   72–5736
ISBN 0-13-329086-7
ISBN 0-13-329078-6 (pbk.)

Printed in the United States of America

10 9 8 7 6 5 4 3 2 1

PRENTICE-HALL INTERNATIONAL, INC., LONDON
PRENTICE-HALL OF AUSTRALIA, PTY. LTD., SYDNEY
PRENTICE-HALL OF CANADA, LTD., TORONTO
PRENTICE-HALL OF INDIA PRIVATE LIMITED, NEW DELHI
PRENTICE-HALL OF JAPAN, INC., TOKYO

For Merry and Helen

Editor's Note

Language permeates human interaction, culture, behavior, and thought. The *Foundations of Modern Linguistics Series* focuses on current research in the nature of language.

Linguistics as a discipline has undergone radical change within the last decade. Questions raised by today's linguists are not necessarily those asked previously by traditional grammarians or by structural linguists. Most of the available introductory texts on linguistics, having been published several years ago, cannot be expected to portray the colorful contemporary scene. Nor is there a recent book surveying the spectrum of modern linguistic research, probably because the field is still moving too fast, and no one author can hope to capture the diverse moods reflected in the various areas of linguistic inquiry. But it does not seem unreasonable now to ask individual specialists to provide a picture of how they view their own particular field of interest. With the *Foundations of Modern Linguistics Series* we will attempt to organize the kaleidoscopic present-day scene. Teachers in search of up-to-date materials can choose individual volumes of the series for courses in linguistics and in the nature of language.

If linguistics is no longer what it was ten years ago its relation to other disciplines has also changed. Language is peculiarly human and it is found deep inside the mind. Consequently, the problems of modern linguistics are equally of concern to anthropology, sociology, psychology, and philosopy. Linguistics has always had a close affiliation with literature and with foreign language learning. Developments in other areas have had their impact on linguistics. There are mathematical models of language and formalisms of its structure. Computers are being used to test grammars. Other sophisticated instrumentation has revolutionized research in phonetics. Advances in neurology have contributed to our understanding of language pathologies and to the development of language. This series is also intended, then, to acquaint other disciplines with the progress going on in linguistics.

Finally, we return to our first statement. Language permeates our lives. We sincerely hope that the *Foundations of Modern Linguistics Series* will be of interest to anyone wanting to know what language is and how it affects us.

Sanford A. Schane, *editor*

Contents

Preface   *xv*

Phase Structure   *1*

Background   **1.1**   *1*

Phrase Structure Grammars   **1.2**   *7*

Classes of Grammars and Generative Capacity   **1.3**   *13*

Formal Models of the Grammars of Natural Languages   *18*

Preliminary Remarks   **2.1**   *18*

Dependencies in Regular Languages   **2.2**   *19*

English as a Nonfinite State Language   **2.3**   *22*

Universal Grammar and Generative Capacity   **2.4**   *26*

The Formal Construction of Transformations

The Motivation for Transformational Analysis 3.1   29

Structural Descriptions 3.2   35

Structural Changes 3.3   41

The Condition on Recoverability of Deletions 3.4   48

Conventions for the Application of Transformations 3.5   50

Constraints on Grammars and Generative Capacity

57

Preliminary Remarks 4.1   57

Universal Grammar and the Problem of Child Language Acquisition 4.2   60

The Standard Theory 4.3   63

The Evaluation Metric 4.4   68

THE STRUCTURE OF SIMPLICITY 4.4.1   68

GENERAL CHARACTERISTICS OF EVALUATION METRICS 4.4.2   69

THE ROLE OF SIMPLICITY IN THE ANALYSIS OF THE ENGLISH AUXILIARY 4.4.3   72

Formal Deductive Systems

76

Introduction 5.1   76

The Propositional Calculus 5.2   77

THE LANGUAGE FOR PROPOSITIONAL CALCULUS 5.2.1   77

TRUTH TABLES 5.2.2   78

DERIVATIONS IN PROPOSITIONAL LOGIC 5.2.3 *85*

TRANSFORMATIONAL DEDUCTIONS 5.2.4 *90*

General Properties of Computation Systems **5.3** *103*

The First-Order Predicate Calculus **5.4** *105*

A LANGUAGE FOR *FPC* 5.4.1 *106*

INTERPRETATIONS FOR *LPC* 5.4.2 *110*

Three Theories of Semantics   *116*

Introduction **6.1** *116*

The Theory of Syntactic Structures **6.2** *117*

The *Aspects* Theory **6.3** *119*

Alternatives to the Standard Theory **6.4** *122*

Bibliography   *127*

Preface

The theory of linguistic structure first presented in Chomsky's monumental unpublished *The Logical Theory of Linguistic Structure*, and modified later in his *Aspects of the Theory of Syntax*, has never received published treatment in its full form. Rather, this theory of syntax has seeped through the seams of various papers on syntax and the theory of syntax, and has been passed by word of mouth from linguist to linguist, receiving variously accurate renderings at each retelling. Linguistics has become in several essential aspects like the oral tradition of the Indian grammarians, except that the attention to detail of Panini is nowhere evidenced.

It is my intention to place into written form, accessible to the reader with no previous training in linguistics, an account of the main features of Chomsky's theory of syntax. I hope that an account of this theory will be of more than historical interest, despite the rapid developments in linguistic theory since the publication of *Aspects* in 1965. The theory discussed in this book has served in most cases as a yardstick against which various proposed innovations have been measured, although frequently the measurement is to be stated in units of distance from the theory.

xv

Perhaps the only generally shared point of agreement concerning the Chomsky theory is that it is inadequate as a theory of universal grammar. At the same time, it is now almost impossible to gauge the historical importance of this theory, both within the field of linguistics and in such related disciplines as psychology.

Perhaps the greatest contribution of Chomsky's theory of grammar is that it adds a new metaphysic, as it were, to the study of language. The theory says that the acquisition of language may be treated, in part, in terms of the internalization of certain combinatorial routines involved in the construction and, perhaps, interpretation of sentences of a natural language. The step between primary linguistic experience and knowledge of the particular grammatical processes of a language is mediated by the child's genetically endowed capacities for learning language—his knowledge of universal grammar. The combinatorial processes of sentence formation contain mechanisms which provide for the arbitrarily large number of different sentences found in any natural language.

The text is organized into three parts. The first two chapters concern the organization of phrase structure grammars and the inherent limitations of these as devices of linguistic description. Chapters 3 and 4 deal with transformational processes and the nature of grammatical constraints. The last two chapters deal with semantics. Chapter 5 is devoted to developing traditional formal logic in terms of notions proper to transformational syntax developed earlier in the text. In this chapter the general theory of computation systems is outlined. The final chapter contains a sketch of three theories of the semantics of natural language developed within the transformational framework.

John P. Kimball

Santa Cruz, California
Jai Guru Dev

Phrase Structure

Background

Linguistics undertakes the study of human language by means of a study of the grammars of particular languages, for the purpose of arriving at a specification of the form which any such grammar may assume. The interaction between the theory of grammar and the construction of particular grammars is necessarily complex, but such interaction between data and theory is to be expected in an empirical science. In order to understand the linguistic enterprise, it is necessary to understand what is meant by *language* and *grammar of a language.*

Given some finite set of symbols, V (the vocabulary), a language L over V is a set of finite strings of symbols drawn from V. Although V is finite by definition, L may be finite or infinite. For example, if V is the set

$\{a, b, c\}$, then the set of strings $\{abc, acb, bac, bca, cab, cba\}$ is a finite language over V. The set of strings of the form $\{abc, abbc, abbbc, \ldots\}$ is an infinite language over V. The set $\{a, b, c\}$, i.e., V itself, is counted as a language over V by the definition above. The set of strings $\{abc, adc\}$ is not a language over V, because one string of symbols in this set contains a symbol not in V. Finally, we conventionally count the *null* language, the language with no strings, as a language over V for any vocabulary V. The strings in a language L are also known as the *sentences* of L.

If V is a vocabulary (i.e., a finite set), then it is convenient to denote the set of all strings of length i over V by V^i. That is, if V is taken as above, then $V^1 = V = \{a, b, c\}$; $V^2 = \{aa, ab, ac, bb, ba, bc, cc, ca, cb\}$; and so on. Then V^* is the union of V^i for all i; i.e., V^* is the set of all finite strings of symbols drawn from V.

A *grammar* of a language L is some finite specification of the sentences of L. If L is a finite language, then L itself can be considered as a grammar of L; we might call this the *list grammar* of L. If L is an infinite language, however, the grammar of L must be some means of specifying the constituency of L other than a list, since grammars are finite objects. A great deal more will be said later about the internal construction of grammars; for the time being it is sufficient to note that although languages may be infinite, grammars of languages must be finite.

Let us see how the above terminology is applied to the case of a natural language like English. The vocabulary, V, is simply a list of words of English. (Note that a dictionary is more than a vocabulary, since a dictionary gives definitions as well as providing a list of lexical items.) English is the set of finite strings, consisting of the grammatical sentences, over this vocabulary. Thus, the string 'the ant saw the anteater' is in English as it is grammatical, but 'ant the saw anteater the' is not. English is an infinite language, which can be seen by considering examples such as the following:

(1) *Two plus two is four, and three plus three is six, and* . . . .

(2) *If two plus two is four, then if three plus three is six, then if* . . . , *then the moon is green cheese.*

(3) *George knows a man that saw a girl that loves a boy that* . . . .

(4) *It surprised George that it bothered Bill that it disturbed Tom* . . . *that it amused Harry that two plus two is four.*

These examples are but a few of the ways in which it is possible to construct sentences of arbitrary length in English. Since for any integer, n, it is possible to construct a grammatical sentence of English of longer than n words, it follows that English is an infinite language. Further, the mechanisms illustrated above for building arbitrarily long sentences are found in all languages, so each natural language is an infinite language.

If V be taken as the vocabulary for English, then it is clear that English is not all of V^*, because not all strings of English words are grammatical sentences of English. The grammar of English must, then, select from all of V^* those strings which are sentences of English.

We will turn now to the matter of organization of strings of symbols into phrases, and will establish that the sentences of English in fact exhibit such organization, known as phrase structure.

A string of symbols such as *abc* may be viewed as *a* followed by *b* followed by *c*, as *ab* followed by *c*, or as *a* followed by *bc*. Nothing is said so far concerning the purposes for which such a string might be viewed in such ways; it is sufficient to note that different hierarchical organizations can be imposed on a given string. It is customary to indicate the hierarchical organization of a string by means of brackets. Using this notation, the possible ways of breaking the string *abc* into phrases would be [a][b][c], [ab][c], and [a][bc]. Two conventions limit the possibilities for breaking up a string into phrases. First, no symbol or substring of symbols may belong to two different phrases at the same time. Thus, the string *abc* cannot be broken up into *ab* followed by *bc*, since the symbol *b* would then belong to two different phrases. Second, only a string of adjacent symbols can constitute a phrase. Thus, the string *abc* could not be parsed into a string *a . . . c* and *b*, for *a* and *c* are not adjacent symbols and thus cannot alone constitute a phrase. In breaking up a string into phrases, every symbol is a member of some phrase, even if that phrase contains that symbol alone.

A way of representing the phrase structure of strings of symbols other than bracketing employs what is known as a *tree diagram*. The different ways of breaking up *abc* indicated above would be represented by tree diagrams as follows:

(1) 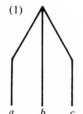 (2)  (3)

The point from which lines branch is called a *node*. A node may branch into any number of lines, including a single one. In diagram (1) there are four nodes, the top node, which branches into three lines, and the three intermediate nodes, each of which branches into one line. A way of parsing *abc* not mentioned above is shown by (4).

(4)

In this parsing, the whole string is represented as one phrase. The difference between (4) and (1) is that the former represents the string as one phrase of three symbols, while the latter represents the string as a phrase which consists of a sequence of three phrases, each of which consists of one symbol. In the bracketing notation, (4) would be represented as [*abc*].

The first convention mentioned above concerning the construction of well-formed parsings of a string prohibits tree diagrams like (5). The second convention disallowing discontinuous substrings from being counted as a single phrase prohibits tree diagrams like (6), where lines connecting parts of a phrase to nodes cross. Finally, the stipulation that every symbol in a string be the member of some phrase in a well-formed parsing counts a tree diagram like (7) as illegal, for there is a symbol to which no line is attached.

(5)   (6)   (7)

In parsing strings of symbols in a language, it is possible to label the phrase structure nodes of the parsed string. This labeling is indicated by writing the label over the node. For example, attaching arbitrary labels to the nodes in (1)–(4), we arrive at (1')–(4').

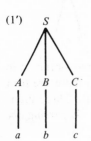   

(1')   (2')   (3')   (4')

The difference between (3) and (4) is perhaps clearer when the nodes are labeled, as in (1') and (4'). When trees such as (1')–(4') are written out using brackets, the labels on nodes are attached to corresponding brackets; the result is called a *labeled bracketing*. Tree diagrams (1')–(4') would be written as follows:

(1') $[_S[_A a]_A [_B b]_B [_C c]_C]_S$

(2') $[_S[_A [ab]_A c]_S$

(3') $[_S a[_B bc]_B]_S$

(4') $[_S abc]_S$

Notice that since any phrase in a parsed string may be dominated by an arbitrary number of nodes, it is possible to associate with each string an indefinitely large number of different parsings. This can, perhaps, be best illustrated by considering a string of length one. With such a string, say *a*, we can associate an infinite number of trees, as shown below.

(8)

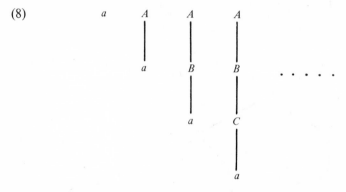

For reasons concerning the generation of trees by phrase structure grammars, to be discussed later, node labels are called *nonterminal symbols;* they are denoted by *A*, *B*, *C*, ... The symbols with which the sentences of a language are constructed are called *terminal symbols*. In a certain sense terminal symbols are also node labels, but the nodes they label are terminal nodes in the sense that such nodes never branch. Terminal symbols are denoted *a*, *b*, *c*, ... Let us now introduce a slight revision in terminology. The vocabulary for a language, *V*, will be taken to include both the terminal symbols which make up the sentences of a language and the nonterminal symbols which label the nodes of parsed terminal strings. This enlarged *V* will consist of two disjoint sets: V_T of terminal symbols (the old *V*), and V_N of nonterminal symbols.

Let us now apply to natural language some of the notions developed in abstraction. In particular, we will see that it is necessary to deal with sentences of natural language as labeled bracketings rather than merely strings of lexical items without phrase structure.

Notice, first, that in certain cases the different meanings of an ambiguous sentence are correlated with different phrase structures for that sentence. To take a now classic example, a sentence like 'They are flying planes' has two possible meanings, depending on its phrase structure. The different parsings would be:

(9)

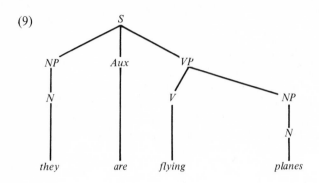

$$S = sentence$$
$$NP = noun\ phrase$$
$$Aux = auxiliary$$
$$V = verb$$
$$N = noun$$
$$Adj = adjective$$

(10)

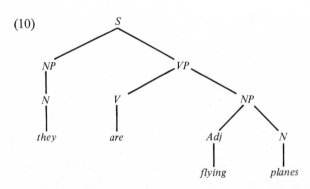

If the grammar of English went no farther than to represent the fact that 'They are flying planes' as a string of words is grammatical in English, it would provide an inadequate model of the intuitions of speakers concerning this sentence. In order to account correctly for the ambiguity in this sentence, the grammar must make crucial use of phrase structure.

The second example showing that the grammar of English must make essential reference to the phrase structure of sentences rather than simply to words in serial order concerns the formation of questions. In a sentence like (11a), the word 'have' is placed in front of the sentence to form the question (11b).

(11)   a. *The centaur has frightened the unicorn.*
       b. *Has the centaur frightened the unicorn?*

In a sentence like (12a), in which there are two occurrences of the word 'have,' only the first is moved to the front in questions; if the second is moved, the ungrammatical sentence (12c) results. (Ungrammatical sentences are so indicated with an asterisk.)

(12) a. *They have said that we have finished the score.*
      b. *Have they said that we have finished the score?*
      c. **Have they have said that we finished the score?*

Such examples suggest that the process that forms such questions must be restricted to moving the first 'have' of a sentence. Sentences like (13), however, show that such an approach will not invariably work.

(13) a. *The fact that the centaur has finished has frightened the unicorn.*
      b. *Has the fact that the centaur has finished frightened the unicorn?*
      c. **Has the fact that the centaur finished has frightened the unicorn?*

In (13a) we formed the question (13b) by moving the second 'have' to the front of the sentence.

The point of such examples is that the process which forms questions in English cannot simply refer to some position in a string of words for finding the right 'have' to move to the front of the sentence. This process must have essential reference to the phrase structure of English sentences; in the cases above it must pick the 'have' that is dominated by the highest *S*-node in the sentence, i.e., the 'have' of the main sentence.

EXERCISES FOR SECTION 1.1

1. Draw six different phrase structure trees for the following terminal string: *abcdefg*.

2. Show how the ambiguity in a phrase like 'old men and women' can be represented as a difference in phrase structure.

3. Show that no matter how the process that changes a sentence like 'John saw the bird' into 'The bird was seen by John' is to be stated, it must make crucial reference to the phrase structure of the sentence to which it applies.

1.2

Phrase Structure Grammars

Grammars are finite devices for specifying languages. In the following we will be concerned with the construction of a class of grammars known as *phrase structure grammars.* Grammars of this sort have the property of delimiting sets of terminal strings, and assigning to each string in the delimited set some phrase structure. We begin by defining the notion of a rule in very general terms.

Given the set of all finite strings over V (where V contains nonterminal as well as terminal symbols), a *rule* over V is a means of effectively pairing strings in this set. Extentionally speaking, a rule is a set of pairs of strings. The word "effective" above is to be taken to mean that, given any two strings from V^*, there is a mechanical procedure for calculating whether these two strings are related by a given rule.

Let us consider two examples. One rule might contain pairs of strings such as: ABc, cBA; $AAcd$, $dcAA$; abc, cba; and so on. This rule relates pairs of strings which are mirror images of each other. (The usual notation is that if x is a string, then x^* denotes its mirror image.) Indeed, there is a finite calculation procedure for determining whether one string is the mirror image of another. Speaking metaphorically, we might say that the rule discussed above "operated" on a string x to produce its reflection x^*.

Consider second a rule which relates pairs like AbC, abC; BAC, BaC; and CdA, Cda. The rule relating pairs in this case is that the first string should have an A someplace in it, while the second string has an a in the corresponding place. Again, speaking metaphorically, we could say that this rule replaces A with a; this is in fact the usual locution.

Phrase structure rules are defined by certain constraints on pairs of strings that can be related by such rules. They are thus called because it is possible to assign a unique phrase structure to strings produced by these rules, but we will return to this later. In defining phrase structure rules, the metaphor alluded to above will be employed for convenience.

When a phrase structure rule applies to a string (the first member of some pair related by the rule), it applies by replacing exactly one nonterminal by some string in V^*. The second rule noted above is a phrase structure rule which replaces A by a. Another example might be that of a rule that replaced C by $abDeF$; pairs of strings like $aBBC$, $aBBabCeF$ would be related by this rule. The usual notation for phrase structure rules is to write an arrow between the string containing nonterminal "being replaced" and the string which replaces it. Thus, the two rules above would be written $\varphi A\psi \to \varphi a\psi$ and $\varphi C\psi \to \varphi abDeF\psi$, respectively, where φ and ψ stand for the environment surrounding the nonterminal.

A phrase structure rule cannot operate to erase some nonterminal symbol. Formally, such an operation could be represented by a rule which replaced a nonterminal by the "null" or "empty" string, and the rule would relate strings like $AbbC$, bbC and aAb, ab. Such a rule is, by definition, not a phrase structure rule. Notice that it follows from this that if X and Y are strings in V^* related by a phrase structure rule, then Y is at least as long as X.

We can now begin to define the notion of a phrase structure grammar, for such a grammar is, in part, a collection of phrase structure rules, finite in number. Given a grammar G, with rules $R = r_1, \ldots, r_n$, then a *derivation* in G is a sequence of strings from V^*, $s_1, \ldots, s_k$, such that adjacent strings, s_i, s_{i+1}, are related by some rule, r_j, in R. Each string in a derivation is called a *line* of that derivation. For example, given a grammar with a set of rules as in (14), then (15) would be a derivation in that grammar:

(14)   (i) $\varphi A \psi \rightarrow \varphi BC \psi$ (15) $A\quad C\quad C\quad A$ (i)

    (ii) $\varphi B \psi \rightarrow \varphi BAc\psi$ $BC\quad C\quad C\quad A$ (iii)

    (iii) $\varphi C \psi \rightarrow \varphi c \psi$ $BC\quad c\quad C\quad A$ (ii)

                               $BAcC\quad c\quad C\quad A$

Given a rule of the form $\varphi A \psi \rightarrow \varphi X \psi$, where X is any string in V^*, we say that this rule *rewrites* A as X. If a string of a derivation contains more than one A, the rule cannot be applied to convert all of these to X simultaneously; a rule applies to only one nonterminal at any point in a derivation. However, by a sequence of applications, it will be possible to replace all occurrences of A by X. For example, the lines in (16a) are not a derivation in the above grammar (or in any grammar), for rule (iii) applied at several points at one time; (16b), however, is a possible derivation in the grammar.

(16) (a) $A\quad C\quad C\quad A$ (iii)   (b) $A\quad C\quad C\quad A$ (iii)

        $A\quad c\quad c\quad A$ $A\quad c\quad C\quad A$ (iii)

                                  $A\quad c\quad c\quad A$

If a derivation is considered as a way of getting from the initial string to the final string by means of a series of rules, then in certain cases this may be done in more than one way. In (16b) the initial string was $ACCA$ and the final string $AccA$; however, a different derivation, (16c), can effect the same transition.

(c) $A\quad C\quad C\quad A$ (iii)

    $A\quad C\quad c\quad A$ (iii)

    $A\quad c\quad c\quad A$

In some sense derivations (16b, c) may be considered equivalent, for they differ only in the order in which rules were applied to different parts of the string. Let us say informally that derivations are to be considered to be equivalent when they differ only as (16b, c) differ.

Let us see how it is possible to assign phrase markers to final strings of derivations using the notion of equivalent derivation outlined above. The first convention for doing this is that if a rule $\varphi A \psi \rightarrow \varphi X \psi$ applies in a derivation, then the string X is to be traced to a node labeled A. If we apply this convention to derivation (15), we arrive at the following configuration, where the lines are drawn in the usual way to indicate phrasing.

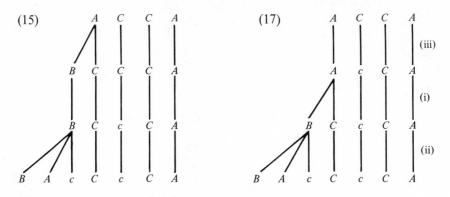

(15)   (17)

                                                                              (iii)

                                                                              (i)

                                                                              (ii)

Notice that (15) and (17) differ as diagrams. However, if we now apply a convention to erase superfluous nodes, then (15) and (17) become the same, namely (18). (We define "superfluous node" here to be any node which is uniquely dominated by itself.)

(18)

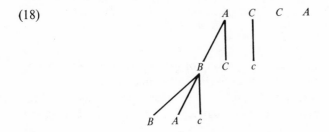

By the convention for constructing pruned phrase trees, equivalent derivations define the same trees. These are also called phrase markers. It can be seen that the phrase structure imposed on the final string of a derivation is the product of the ways the rules applied in the derivation. It is also evident that if we relaxed the convention that phrase structure rules can rewrite only one symbol, there would be no natural way to assign phrase structure to derived strings. That is, suppose we allowed some rule to rewrite two symbols, say BC, at once. The rule would then be written $\varphi BC\psi \rightarrow \varphi X\psi$, and two adjacent strings might look like $AAacBCd$, $AAacXd$, where X is some element of V^*. The string X would not in this case be dominated by a node, for B and C are labels of two adjacent nodes; thus, we could not assign X to any phrase node without some ad hoc device (e.g., to assign it always to the leftmost node).

Given the above notion of derivation, we can complete the definition of the class of phrase structure grammars. For this we need two ancillary definitions: Let Σ be some subset of V_N, i.e., a set of nonterminals. Then a Σ-*derivation* is a derivation which begins with one of the symbols from Σ. In linguistics we let Σ consist of the symbol S (sentence) alone. Second, we define a *terminated derivation* to be one whose last line consists only of terminal symbols. A *phrase structure grammar* consists of a set of rules, R, all of which are phrase structure rules as defined above; a vocabulary, V, consisting of a set of nonterminals, V_N, and a set of terminals, V_T, where V_N and V_T have no members in common; and a subset of V_N, Σ. The *strong generative capacity* of a grammar, G, is the set of trees of equivalence classes of terminated Σ-derivations generated by the rules of that grammar. The *weak generative capacity* of G is the set of terminal strings which appear as last lines of Σ-derivations in G. This latter set is denoted by $L(G)$, read "the language generated by G." The set of trees generated by G may be denoted by $L_S(G)$.

The notions presented above can be explicated by the following example: Let the grammar, G, have vocabulary $V = \{S, A, B, a, b\}$; rules $R = \{\varphi S\psi \rightarrow \varphi AS\psi,\ \varphi A\psi \rightarrow \varphi a\psi,\ \varphi S\psi \rightarrow \varphi AB\psi,\ \varphi B\psi \rightarrow \varphi AB\psi,\ \varphi B\psi \rightarrow \varphi b\psi\}$ where $\Sigma = \{S\}$. The derivation represented in tree form by (19a) is not a Σ-derivation, and that represented by (19b) is not a terminated derivation.

(19)   (a)   (b)

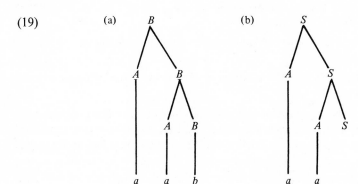

Both (20a, b) are terminated Σ-derivations.

(20)   (a)   *S*   (b)   *S*

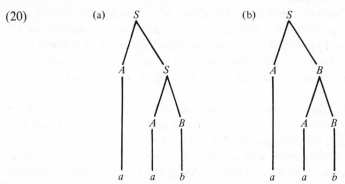

Notice that the terminal string of both of these derivations is the same;
however, this string is assigned different parsings according to the way it was
derived in the grammar. Such a string in $L(G)$ is called *structurally ambiguous*
(or just *ambiguous*).

Now let us form G' from G above by dropping the rule $\varphi S\psi \rightarrow \varphi A S\psi$.
It is evident that $L(G') = L(G)$; that is, these grammars generate the same
set of terminal strings. For every place that the rule deleted in G' was applied
in some derivation in G, we can apply the rule $\varphi S\psi \rightarrow \varphi A B\psi$ in G', to get
the same terminal string. Equally evident is the fact that $L_S(G') \neq L_S(g)$,
since G will generate trees like both (20a, b), whereas G' will only generate
trees like (20b). Thus, we have a case in which the weak generative capacity
of two grammars is the same, while their strong generative capacity differs,
showing that these notions pertain to essentially different aspects of phrase
structure grammars.

EXERCISES FOR SECTION 1.2

1. Construct a grammar whose language is empty; whose language is
finite; whose language is infinite.

2. Find grammars for the following languages: *aaa, aaaba, aaabaaaba,*
. . . ; *acb, accb, acccb, ...*

3. Let $V_T = \{a, b, c\}$. Construct a grammar whose weak generative
capacity is all of V_T^*.

4. Construct a grammar: with a finite number of terminal strings with
structural ambiguities; with an infinite number of strings with structural
ambiguities; with at least one string with an infinite number of structural
ambiguities.

5. Let us say that a nonterminal symbol of a grammar is *recursive* if
that symbol may dominate a subtree in a derivation in which another

occurrence of the same symbol is contained. That is, a symbol, A, is recursive if in some tree generated by the grammar we can find an occurrence of A, and then by tracing downwards along lines of tree domination find another occurrence of A. Show that if the language generated by a grammar is infinite, then that grammar contains at least one recursive symbol.

1.3

Classes of Grammars
and Generative Capacity

Grammars are classified according to the sorts of rules they contain. We have given a general characterization of phrase structure rules without discussing the possible varieties of such rules. We will now define classes of rules according to their formal properties, later extending this definition to classify grammars.

As discussed above, the general form of a phrase structure rule is $\varphi A\psi \to \varphi X\psi$, where φ and ψ provide the context in which A may be rewritten as X. For example, a rule of the form $BAC \to BXC$ says that A is to be rewritten as X in the environment B_C. Such a rule, also written $A \to X/B\_C$, is called a *context sensitive rule*. It is possible, however, for a rule to rewrite A as X in any environment φ_ψ; such a rule is called a *context free rule*. Since no environment restricts application of the rule, specification of the environment may be omitted, and the rule written $A \to X$.

Just as a context free rule is a special kind of context sensitive rule (in which the context is null), *regular rules* are special kinds of context free rules. A regular rule is a rule such as $A \to a$, or of the form $A \to Bc$ or $A \to cB$. The former kind are called *left-branching* rules, while those of the latter sort are called *right-branching*. This terminology originates in the fact that if rules of the first kind are applied to form a tree, as in (21a), the resulting structure is left-branching; right-branching rules produce a structure like (21b).

(21)

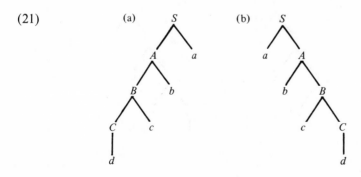

A *context sensitive grammar* is a grammar which contains at least one context sensitive rule. A *context free grammar* contains only context free rules. A *regular grammar* contains rules exclusively of the form $A \rightarrow Bc$, $A \rightarrow a$, or of the form $A \rightarrow cB$, $A \rightarrow a$. Regular grammars are thus classified as left- or right-branching according to the kind of rules they contain. A *context sensitive language* is a language generated by a context sensitive grammar; similarly, *context free languages* are generated by context free grammars, and *regular languages* by regular grammars. Henceforth, we use *CS* for context sensitive, *CF* for context free, and *R* for regular.

We turn next to considerations of generative capacity. Given some class of grammars, C, its *generative capacity* is defined as the set of languages generated by grammars in that class. Given two classes of grammars, C_1 and C_2, the generative capacity of C_1, say, is said to be greater than that of C_2 if every language generable by some grammar in C_2 is also generable by a grammar in C_1, but not conversely.

Let us apply these notions to right-branching and left-branching regular grammars. For convenience, we will write a regular grammar as G_R if it is right-branching, and G_L if it is left-branching. It will be shown that the generative capacity of the class of G_R's is the same as that of the class of G_L's. That is, if some language L is $L(G_R)$ for some G_R, then there exists a G_L such that $L = L(G_L)$. To show this it is necessary to introduce a definition and prove a preliminary lemma. If L is a language, then define L^* to be the set of mirror images of strings in L; i.e., L^* is the set of x^*, such that x is a string in L.

L e m m a

If L is generated as $L(G_L^1)$, for some left-branching grammar G_L^1, then there is a left-branching grammar G_L^2 such that $L^* = L(G_L^2)$.

Proof: The proof consists of showing that there is a procedure for turning derivations of G_L^1 around to make the initial symbol the final symbol in derivations in G_L^2, and conversely. Thus, if (22a) is a sample derivation in G_L^1, G_L^2 will contain a corresponding derivation (22b).

(22)   (a)   (b)

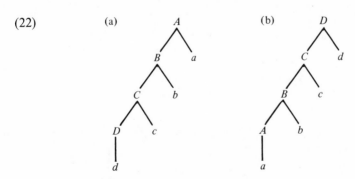

It is possible to see how rules of G_L^2 are constructed from those of G_L^1. If X is an arbitrary nonterminal, and x an arbitrary terminal, then: (i) if $A \rightarrow Bx$ and $B \rightarrow Xb$ are rules of G_L^1, then $B \rightarrow Ab$ will be a rule of G_L^2; (ii) if $D \rightarrow Xe$ is in G_L^1, where D is an initial symbol, then $D \rightarrow e$ is in G_L^2; (iii) the initial symbols of G_L^2 will be all those nonterminals, X, where $X \rightarrow x$ is a rule of G_L^1.

By this procedure, rules which generate (22a), namely the rules in (23a), will be converted to rules in (23b), which generate (23b).

(23) (a) $A \rightarrow Ba$ (b) $D \rightarrow Cd$ by (i)

        $B \rightarrow Cb$ $C \rightarrow Bc$ by (i)

        $C \rightarrow Dc$ $B \rightarrow Ab$ by (i)

        $D \rightarrow d$ $A \rightarrow a$ by (ii)

D would be an initial symbol in the second grammar above, by convention (iii).

The procedures (i)–(iii) show how a left-branching grammar G_L^1 generating L is to be turned into another left-branching grammar, G_L^2. It remains to be shown that $L(G_L^2) = L^*$. The proof of this involves mathematical induction over the length of derivations in G_L^1, and will be left for the reader with sufficient background.

We are now in a position to establish the following theorem:

Theorem

For every right-branching grammar, G_R, there is a left-branching grammar, G_L, such that $L(G_R) = L(G_L)$.

Proof: In the proof, we first convert G_R into a left-branching grammar, G_L', which generates $L(G_R)^*$. The lemma is then applied to produce a G_L such that $L(G_L) = L(G_L')^* = L(G_R)^{**} = L(G_R)$.

G_R is converted to G_L by changing every rule in G_R of the form $A \rightarrow cB$ to a rule of the form $A \rightarrow Bc$. Thus, a derivation like (24a) in G_R would appear as the backwards derivation (24b) in G_L'.

(24)

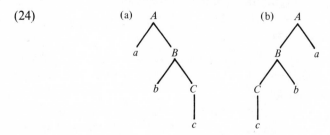

It is now obvious that the language of G'_L is the set of mirror images of the language of the original G_R. (A rigorous proof would involve mathematical induction over the length of derivations in G_R.) Applying the lemma, we produce from G'_L a grammar G_L whose language is that of G_R.

The above theorem proves half of what is needed; it remains to be shown that for every left-branching grammar there is a right-branching grammar with the same language. The proof proceeds as above, with a corresponding lemma; it is left as an exercise.

The above result establishes that the class of right-branching R grammars and the class of left-branching R grammars have the same weak generative capacity. On the other hand, they do not have identical strong generative capacities, since grammars in the respective classes assign right- versus left-branching structures to terminal strings.

Since R grammars are species of CF grammars, the generative capacity of the former is clearly contained in that of the latter. In fact, the class of CF grammars have a greater generative capacity than that of the class of R grammars. The proof of this proceeds by constructing a language generated by a CF grammar, but not generated by any R grammar. The construction of such a language will be carried out in the next chapter. There is also a CS language not generable by any CF grammar, and thus the generative capacity of the CS grammars is greater than that of the CF grammars.

Let us define an *unrestricted rewrite system* (*URS*) as one in which we allow symbols to be erased in the course of a derivation. Then, it is possible to show that there are languages generated by *URS*'s not generable by CS grammars, and thus perforce not by CF or R grammars.

The hierarchy of classes of grammars described above, arranged according to increasing generative capacity, is known as the *Chomsky hierarchy*. Proceeding from bottom to top, the elements of this hierarchy are the R grammars, CF grammars, CS grammars, and *URS*'s. It has been shown (Kimball, 1967) that the class of *URS*'s have the same generative capacity as the class of transformational grammars, under the definition given in Chomsky (1965). It will be discussed later why such an equivalence in generative capacity is to be taken as showing that linguistics has not as yet been able to construct a fully adequate theory of grammar.

EXERCISES FOR SECTION 1.3

1. Construct a right-branching R grammar generating a language of the form *ab, abc, abcdcd, abcdcdcd, ...* Now construct a left-branching grammar to generate this language.

2. Prove the converse of the theorem above: For every left-branching R grammar there is a right-branching R grammar with the same language.

3. Construct a *CS* grammar which generates a language of the form *abc*, *aabbcc*, *aaabbbccc*, . . . (in general $a^n b^n c^n$, *n* an integer). (Hint: Construct rules which will generate nonterminal strings of the form *ABC*, *ABCABC*, *ABCABCABC*, . . . , i.e., $[ABC]^n$. Then write some *CS* rules to move all *A*'s to the left and all *C*'s to the right, leaving *B*'s in the middle. Then instantiate the nonterminals as terminals.)

4. Construct a *CF* grammar which will generate strings of the form *abc*, *aabcc*, *aaabccc*, . . . (i.e., $a^n b c^n$).

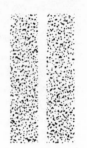

Formal Models
of the Grammars
# of Natural Languages

Preliminary Remarks

Chapter One introduced three classes of formal grammars. The mathematical study of these grammars consists largely in the specification of formal properties of the languages generated by them. The linguist takes these formal grammars as possible first approximations to models of the grammars of natural languages, i.e., devices which generate natural languages and whose internal structure is the same as that of grammars of adult speakers.

As in any science in which a formal object is presented as a possible model of an empirical phenomenon, one is concerned in linguistics with properties of the formal model in question. For example, if regular grammars are posited as candidates for grammars of natural languages, and if some general theorem has been proved establishing that regular languages have particular properties, then we would predict that natural languages have the properties in question.

This chapter deals with the question of whether regular languages could serve as models for the grammars of natural languages. We will first prove an important theorem characterizing regular languages, and will then compare the properties of regular languages established by this theorem with certain facts about one natural language, English. This discussion is essentially that in Chapter 3 of Chomsky (1957), to which the reader is referred. It bears repetition in greater detail, however, as Chomsky's discussion is sketchy in places and invites misunderstanding.

There is a great deal to be learned from this microcosmic exercise in linguistic theory building. We will discover, with Chomsky, that regular grammars are inadequate in fundamental respects as formal models of grammars of natural languages. What is to be gained from consideration of questions of this sort is an understanding of a fundamental technique of research in linguistics.

2.2

Dependencies in Regular Languages

In this section we will be concerned with proving a general theorem characterizing a certain property of all regular languages. This theorem says, in effect, that regular languages are limited in complexity in an important respect. We will see in the next section that this limitation excludes regular languages from being possible models of the grammars of natural languages.

It should be remarked first that the regular languages with which we will be dealing are provably identical to those languages generated (accepted) by what are known as finite state machines (to be discussed below). We have chosen to deal with regular (finite state) languages by means of grammars rather than machines only for reasons of ease of exposition.

The sort of complexity of interest here involves what are called dependencies. Let $S = a_1 \ldots a_n$ be a sentence of some language, L, and let b_1, b_2 be terminal symbols. We say that S has a (b_1, b_2) dependency if it is the case that whenever $b_1 = a_i$, for some i, then for some j, $i < j$, it must be the case that $a_j = b_2$. In other words, S has a (b_1, b_2) dependency if every occurrence of b_1 in S must be matched by a later occurrence of b_2.

The next step is to define what it means for dependencies to be nested. Let S have a (b_1, b_2) dependency and a (b_3, b_4) dependency, where possibly $b_1 = b_3$ and $b_2 = b_4$. Then the latter dependency is *nested* in the former if

b_3 follows b_1 but precedes b_2. Consider, for example, the following possibilities for S:

(1) $a_1 \ldots b_1 \ldots b_2 \ldots b_3 \ldots b_4 \ldots a_n$

(2) $a_1 \ldots b_1 \ldots b_3 \ldots b_4 \ldots b_2 \ldots a_n$

(3) $a_1 \ldots b_1 \ldots b_3 \ldots b_2 \ldots b_4 \ldots a_n$

(4) $a_1 \ldots b_3 \ldots b_4 \ldots b_1 \ldots b_3 \ldots b_4 \ldots b_2 \ldots a_n$

In (1) the dependency (b_3, b_4) occurs but is not nested in (b_1, b_2). In (2) and (3) (b_3, b_4) is nested in (b_1, b_2), because in both of these b_3 follows b_1 but precedes b_2. In (4) the first occurrence of (b_3, b_4) is not nested, but the second is nested.

A terminal string has an n-termed nested dependency if it is the case that n initial symbols of dependencies occur before the final symbols of any of these occur. By this definition, (1) has a 1-termed nested dependency (also called nesting), while (2)–(4) have each 2-termed nestings. Example (5) has a 3-termed nesting.

(5) $a_1 \ldots b_1 \ldots b_1 \ldots b_1 \ldots b_2 \ldots b_2 \ldots b_2 \ldots a_n,$

where (b_1, b_2) is the dependent pair.

Let us say that a grammar, G, *expresses m-termed nested dependencies* if every sentence generated by G with m initial symbols of dependent pairs contains the final symbols of those pairs. The following theorem shows that each regular grammar has an inherent limitation on the nested dependencies which it can express.

Theorem

For every regular grammar G, there is a fixed integer n, such that G cannot express nested dependencies of r terms for any $r \geq n$.

Remark: This theorem does not state that the G in question cannot generate sentences with, say, an $n + 1$ nested dependency, where each initial symbol is followed by its final symbol. It means that G cannot guarantee that *every* sentence with $n + 1$ initial symbols will contain final symbols for each. To clarify the matter further, consider the following example: Let (a, b) be a dependent pair. Let G be a regular grammar that generates strings of the form $a^n b^m$, for all $n, m \neq 0$. G will, in particular, generate strings of the form $a^k b^k$, where each a is paired by exactly one b, but G will also generate strings such as $a^7 b^3$, where not every a is paired by a following b. For this grammar, the integer specified in the theorem is 2, since the string 'ab' correctly expresses the dependency, but the grammar generates 'aab', which fails to match one 'a' with a 'b'.

Proof: Without loss of generality, we restrict our attention to right-branching regular grammars with one dependent pair (b, c). Any such grammar has a nonterminal vocabulary, V_N, with a finite number of symbols, k. Consider a string in which $k + 1$ initial b's occur before any c's occur. Since each terminal symbol in a string generated by a regular grammar is matched by exactly one nonterminal in the tree assigned to the string by derivation in the grammar, some nonterminal, such as A, must occur twice in the generation of the string with $k + 1$ initial b's. The string we are considering has a form represented in (6).

(6)

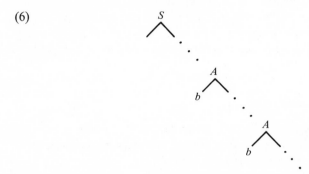

As indicated in (6), in the string under consideration, two occurrences of b among the initial $k + 1$ b's are dominated by the nonterminal A.

Suppose now that the grammar under consideration can complete this string with at least $k + 1$ c's following the $k + 1$ initial b's, to satisfy all the dependencies. In other words, suppose the grammar can generate the string above in which $k + 1$ b's are followed by m c's, where $m \geq k + 1$. Then the second occurrence of A in (6) can dominate a string that contains m c's. Notice now that A is a recursive symbol, and that the grammar can "loop" through an indefinite number of A's, generating an indefinitely large number of b's, before any c is generated. In particular, the grammar can generate a string with more than m initial b's. However, as noted above, it is possible for A to dominate a subtree which contains only m c's. Thus, we have proven at least that the grammar cannot express dependencies of greater than m nested terms.

The proof above has an intuitive content somewhat as follows. A right-branching regular grammar can be thought of as generating a string of left to right. The memory of such a computing device is limited by the size of its nonterminal vocabulary in the following sense: in determining whether to introduce some terminal at a particular point in a derivation, the grammar can remember back in the string only as far as nonterminals different from the one introducing the new terminal occur. Suppose that G is constructed to express an (a, b) dependency. The first time a is introduced dominated by the nonterminal, say, A_1, G goes into what we may term a subroutine which will eventually result in the generation of one b. This subroutine cannot, however, utilize any nonterminal which occurred in the derivation prior to the generation of a, since a cycle could then be set up for the generation of an arbitrarily large number of a's, and the grammar would emit only one b. Suppose now that a second a is produced under the node A_2 before the b to close the first dependency appears (thus resulting in a 2-termed nested dependency). The grammar must now go into a subroutine different from the first subroutine to generate a b to close the dependency set up by the second a. This subroutine cannot utilize any nonterminal produced up to and including A_2, by the same argument given above. It is evident that G must run out of nonterminals after m-nestings for some m, and so cannot express k-nested dependencies for $k \geq m$.

EXERCISES FOR SECTION 2.2

1. Construct a regular grammar generating $a^n b^m$, where $n = m$ if $n \leq 4$ (i.e., this grammar expresses four termed nested $[a, b]$ dependencies, but not nestings of five or greater terms).

2. Show that the following are not regular languages: all strings of the form $a^n b^m$, where (i) $n < m$; (ii) $n = m$; (iii) $n > m$. (Hint: Find the dependencies.)

3. Show that there exists a regular language L with the following property: Defining LL^* to be the set of strings of the form xx^*, where x is a string from L and x^* is the mirror image of x, we have that LL^* is not generated by a regular grammar.

4. Let k be the number of nonterminals in the vocabulary of a regular grammar, G. Show that G cannot express m-termed nested dependencies for m greater than $k/2$ (i.e., $k/2$ fixes the n of the theorem above).

2.3

English as a Nonfinite State Language

This section will begin with a brief discussion of finite state machines, which provide machine representation of regular languages. The topic is worth consideration because traditional treatment of the problem of considering English as a regular language has proceeded in terms of finite state machines.

A finite state machine is a collection of states, $S_1 \ldots S_k$, a finite alphabet, $a, b, c, \ldots$, and a transition function mapping pairs of alphabet members and states into the set of states. The operation of this function will become clear below. Certain states are designated as initial states, while others are designated as final states. The machine may be considered to either read from or write on a tape. If it is thought of as reading, then the set of finite strings on the tape which will take the machine from some initial state to some final state is called the language accepted by the machine. If the machine is thought of as writing on the tape, then the set of finite strings written on the tape when the machine goes from some initial state to some final state, throwing out a symbol at each transition between states, is called the language generated by the machine. It makes no difference whether we consider machines as generating or accepting languages; for convenience we pick the former way of speaking.

A finite state machine operates as follows: The machine starts out in some state, say S_{i_1}, prints a symbol a_{i_1} on the tape and moves to the next state, S_{i_2}. The transition function specifies what symbol may be printed and which state moved to. The machine moves through a sequence of states, $S_{i_1} \ldots S_{i_k}$, printing symbols $a_{i_1} \ldots a_{i_k}$. When the machine gets to a final state, it may stop. As defined above, the language generated by a machine consists of the set of finite strings of symbols printed on the tape when the machine moves from some initial state to some final state.

Some examples may make the concept of a finite state machine clear. A computer is a finite state machine, although large memory capacity allows computers to mimic other kinds of machines within certain limits. A combination lock may also be considered a finite state machine. If the lock has, for example, three digits in its combination, and a specification of whether the dial is to be moved left or right, then the language is finite, consisting of the three digits, to each of which is appended R or L depending on the direction of motion of the dial. Such a lock would have four states: locked, S_1 after the first correct digit, S_2 after the second correct digit, and unlocked.

Finite state machines can be represented pictorially by labeling circles as states, and drawing arrows between states labeled with the symbol generated when the machine passes from one state to the next. For example, the following is the diagram of a finite state machine that generates a language of the form $(ab)^n c (ef)^m g$.

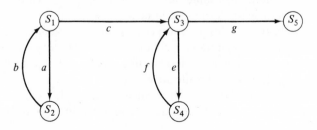

In this machine, the initial state is S_1 and the final state is S_5. Diagrams for finite state machines look like flow charts used in computer programming; indeed, a flow chart is a finite state machine.

Finite state devices are the machine analogs of regular languages, in the sense that the class of languages generated by finite state machines is exactly the class of languages generated by regular grammars. This fact will not be proved formally here, although it is not difficult to indicate the correspondence. The states of the machines correspond to the nonterminals of the grammar. The initial states of machines are initial symbols in the grammar, and the terminal states are nonterminals which occur in a rule of the form $A \rightarrow a$; these are the nonterminals which can terminate the process of derivation, so to speak. If a machine allows transition from state S_i to S_j with the generation of a symbol, a, then a rule of the form $S_i \rightarrow S_j a$ (respectively, $S_i \rightarrow a S_j$ in right-branching grammars) would occur in a grammar generating the same language as that machine. The difference between left- and right-branching grammars is precisely the difference between a machine being thought of as printing symbols on the tape right-to-left or left-to-right, respectively. Given the machine correspondence of regular grammars, the fact that left- and right-branching regular grammars have the same generative capacity becomes obvious. Since finite state devices and regular grammars generate the same languages, the theorem proved in Section 2.1 clearly characterizes finite state languages.

With this background we may consider the question (treated originally in Chomsky, 1957, Chap. 3) of whether English could be generated by finite state machine; i.e., whether English is a finite state language. Equivalently, we may consider whether any regular grammar could serve adequately as a model of the grammar of English. For example, a regular grammar for generating the sentence 'My great aunt went AWOL' might have the rules: $S \rightarrow$ my A, $A \rightarrow$ great B, $B \rightarrow$ aunt C, etc. Correspondingly, a finite state machine to produce this sentence might appear as follows:

Perhaps such a model has some initial plausibility, since words seem to be generated in the machine in the same order in which they come out of the mouth of the speaker. (This appearance is due to the metaphor discussed in the first chapter: grammars and machines are abstract objects and do not "generate" symbols in any order in real time. As formal objects, they simply function to delimit classes of finite strings, called languages.)

It is possible to show that English is in principle excluded from the class of regular (finite state) languages, and thus no regular grammar or finite state machine, regardless of complexity, could generate the grammatical sentences of English. The proof of this, found in Chomsky, consists of showing that English sentences may have m-termed nested dependencies for any m. We draw the examples below from Chomsky (p. 22).

(1) a. *If S_1 then S_2.*
      b. *Either S_3 or S_4.*
      c. *The man who said that S_5 is arriving today.*

Such sentences exhibit dependencies. That is, the 'if' of (1a) must be followed by 'then'; 'either' of (1b) must be followed by 'or', and the verb 'be' must agree with 'man' in (1c) to yield 'is' rather than 'am' or 'are'. These dependencies can be nested without limit, since each of (1a–c) is a sentence and thus can be substituted for S_1-S_5. After a great many nestings the resulting sentence becomes awkward, and pencil and paper might be required to parse the meaning fully due to certain performance limitations on human memory. Such long sentences are to be counted as grammatical in English, however, as the processes whose iteration led to them are central in the formation of shorter and more understandable sentences.

The result is that for any m, there is an English sentence with an m-termed nested dependency. Since for each R grammar, G (finite state machine), there is a fixed m such that G cannot express k-termed nestings for $k \geq m$, any finite state model of English will be inherently incapable of generating all the grammatical sentences.

A stronger conclusion is that no regular grammar can model the competence of a speaker of any language. This conclusion is arrived at from the above discussion by the following line of reasoning: Any regular grammar is inherently incapable of generating English, and thus of modeling the competence of the native English speaker. Part of the competence of the native speaker of English is his ability to form a grammar (the grammar of English) which will generate sentences with m-termed nestings for any m. If the model of universal grammar did not correctly represent the fact that speakers can learn grammars which can express m-termed nestings for any m, then this model would be inadequate. A theory of universal grammar which specified a regular grammar as a possible grammar of a natural language would thus be incorrect.

EXERCISES FOR SECTION 2.3

1. Construct a finite state machine that will generate a language of the form $ab^n cf^m d$.

2. Construct a regular grammar with the above language.

3. There is a construction in English involving the word 'respectively'. Within performance constraints, there seems to be no limit on the number of terms which can be conjoined with 'respectively'. For example, English has sentences like '2, 3, 4, 5, and 6 are less than 3, 4, 5, 6, and 7, respectively'. Can the existence of this construction be used to establish that English is not a finite state language?

4. Using sentences (1a, b, c), construct a sentence having a 5-termed nested dependency.

2.4

**Universal Grammar
and Generative Capacity**

The proof offered in Section 2.1 establishes the existence of a class of languages which are beyond the generative capacity of regular grammars, but which are in general generable by *CF* grammars. These are languages in which sentences exhibit *m*-termed nested dependencies for all *m*. As remarked in Section 1.3, there are also languages beyond the generative capacity of *CF* grammars; for example, a language of the form $a^n b^n c^n$ is generable by a *CS* grammar, but cannot be generated by a *CF* grammar. (See Bar-Hillel, Perles, and Shamir, 1961, for a proof of this.)

The above hierarchy of classes of languages represents the fact that the regular languages are the simplest or least complex, the *CF* languages are next, and the *CS* are the most complex of the phrase structure languages. In a certain sense, the problem faced in the construction of a theory of universal grammar is to determine exactly how "complex" natural language is. The theory of universal grammar must specify the class of grammars which are potential grammars of natural language, and in so doing provide a partial explanation of why any human child, within a normal range of intelligence, can learn something as complex as a natural language within a relatively short period of time, utilizing a set of data limited in scope and not comprising a statistically representative sample of the grammatical sentences of the language.

The theory of grammar can be considered as facing the task of specifying the optimal point along a scale representing the complexity of languages generated by various classes of grammars. If the point is set too low, the languages generated by the class of grammars selected will not be adequate to represent the competence of the native speaker of a language. Thus, selecting the regular grammars as models of the grammars of natural languages would be incorrect, as such grammars cannot generate sentences with *m*-termed nestings for all *m*. On the other hand, to say that the grammar of any natural language is simply a *URS*, i.e., any computation device for producing sentences, would be to make no empirical hypothesis at all. It would add nothing to our knowledge to say that there is some computation procedure for determining whether a string of words is a grammatical sentence in some language, as this is already evidenced by the fact that speakers can perform this task. Further, to say that the grammar of a natural language could be an arbitrary *URS* would leave the problem of child language learning basically unsolved. The class of grammars from which the child could select to produce sentences compatible with the data already presented to him from some language would be unmanageably large, and nothing in such a theory could predict the observed fact that children exposed to different subsets of the same language learn the same grammar.

Thus, the theory of universal grammar must specify a class of grammars as potential grammars of natural language which generate languages, each of which is a potential human language. For example, if we say that a human language is generated by *CS* grammars, then we make the prediction that a language of the form $W_1^n W_2^n W_3^n$ is a potential human language, where W_1, W_2, and W_3 are words. As this hypothesis is patently absurd, we have falsified the above hypothesis. This does not mean that grammars of natural languages could not be drawn from some subclass of the class of *CS* grammars, but the specification of such a subclass would remain to be determined.

Let us define a *grammatical constraint* on some class of grammars, *C*, to be a means of selecting from *C* a subclass of grammars, C_i, such that the generative capacity of C_i is strictly less than that of *C*.

Given a tentative model of universal grammar, i.e., the form of the grammar of any natural language, the model specifies a class of grammars as potential grammars. However, even if every human language could be generated by some grammar in the class, there still may be some languages generated which could not be human languages. The model could be strengthened if the linguist could find some grammatical constraint to select from the class specified by the model a subset of grammars such that (i) every human language could be generated by some grammar in the subset, and (ii) nonhuman languages generated by the larger class would not be generated by the smaller class. By adding empirically justified grammatical constraints to models of universal grammar, the problem of explaining child language learning comes closer to a solution, for we have narrowed the class of grammars from which the child must theoretically select a grammar to fit the data presented him in his native language. The smaller the class of grammar consistent with the presented data, the more reasonable the task of learning the language. The child generalizes from the data of language learning in certain specific ways predicted by the grammar. That is, given certain sentences, the child predicts that other sentences will be grammatical by applying tentatively formulated rules of his grammar. To specify the class of grammars is to explain the generalizations actually observed.

It may be that the most tightly formulated theory of universal grammar specifies a class of grammars such that children learning a language are still faced with numerous potential grammatical models of the language, each consistent with the input data. Selection of a grammar from an array of possibilities is then effected by application of a simplicity metric, which ranks the grammars consistent with some set of data on a scale. Under this hypothesis, the child selects the simplest grammar from the potential grammars consistent with the data.

Linguistic research proceeds, according to the above outline, by placing grammatical constraints on some model of universal grammar. These will restrict the generative capacity of that model, thus bringing us closer to an explanation of child language learning.

Not everything proposed as a "constraint" in the literature is a genuine constraint by the above definition. For example, if a new class of grammars is defined, and that class has a greater generative capacity than the previous model, then the researcher has at least temporarily moved further from the desired explanation of child language learning. Of course, such a move might be justified on independent grounds.

For the reasons sketched above, the proof that the transformational model proposed by Chomsky (1965) is equivalent in weak generative capacity to the class of *URS*'s should be interpreted as indicating that this model is tentative, requiring further grammatical constraints.

EXERCISES FOR SECTION 2.4

Given a language of the form $a^n c b^m$, contrast the different kinds of regular grammars that can be constructed to generate this language versus the different kinds of *CF* grammars to generate the same language.

The Formal Construction
of Transformations

3.1

The Motivation for
Transformational Analysis

In the previous chapter a simple computational model for the grammars of natural languages was investigated. In this chapter we will deal with a more complex model which comes much closer to providing a correct representation of certain grammatical processes. In particular, we will be examining what is known as the transformational component of the grammar of a natural language. Before proceeding with details of the construction of transformations and the conventions for their application, it is worthwhile to discuss the question of the empirical motivation for transformations. In introducing transformations, we will be concerned not only with the generative adequacy of these formal devices, but also with their ability to capture certain generalizations about language.

One may approach the subject of transformations naively by considering that certain sentences of natural language seem to be related to each other in special ways. For example, a sentence like 'The horse threw Dick' bears a relation to 'Dick was thrown by the horse' that it does not bear to 'Dick threw the horse', 'George hit Tom', or 'Seven is a prime number'. Notice that the first two sentences have the same meaning, aside from possible differences of focus or theme, while the first is not synonymous with any of the other sentences. The first sentence does bear certain similarities to both the third and the fourth. It is like the third in containing exactly the same words, with subject and object interchanged, and it is similar to the fourth in form, being a transitive sentence with subject, verb, and direct object. The first sentence is least like the last.

Let us detail the properties of the relation between the first and second sentences, which we may call the *active-passive relationship*, to determine in what ways it is different from the relation between the first and any other of the sample sentences. Notice first that this relation holds between many pairs of sentences, e.g., 'Tom saw a light' and 'A light was seen by Tom', or 'Everyone knew the fact' and 'The fact was known by everyone', but not between 'Tom went to town' and *'The town was gone to by Tom', or 'Jack ate yesterday' and *'Yesterday was eaten by Jack' (although we do have 'Jack ate tomatoes' and 'Tomatoes were eaten by Jack'). In the sentences which enter into this relationship, whatever can occur in object position of the active may appear in subject position of the passive, and whatever may appear in subject position of the active may appear in the *by* phrase of the passive. Thus, whereas 'John saw Bill' is grammatical, *'John saw noon' is not (in the same sense of *see*); correspondingly, 'Bill was seen by John' is grammatical, whereas *'Noon was seen by John' is not. The sentence *'Noon saw Bill' is ungrammatical, as *noon* cannot be the subject of *see*, and the passive form of this sentence, *'Bill was seen by noon', is likewise ungrammatical.

Second, noun phrases (*NP*'s) that never occur in subject position in actives but may occur in object position do appear in subject position in passives. Thus, the 'a good deal' of 'Jack may have known a good deal' never appears independently in subject position, as attested by the ungrammaticality of sentences like *'A good deal walked in the door', *'A good deal weighs three ounces', or *'A good deal is better than bananas'. The 'tabs' of the idiom 'keep tabs on' also never occurs independently in subject position; thus we have *'Tabs was elected president', and *'Tabs proves that two plus two equals four'. However, both of these idiomatic *NP*'s may occur in subject position in passives, e.g., 'A good deal was known by everyone', and 'Tabs were kept on radicals'.

Third, the sentences which enter into the active-passive relationship seem to have characteristic phrase structure configurations. Thus, a sentence like 'John ate yesterday' has no passive form, corresponding to the fact that 'yesterday' in this sentence is an adverb. Corresponding to 'The teddy bear crept into the room' we have no passive *'Into the room was crept by the teddy bear', showing that prepositional phrases (*PP*'s) do not passivize. Note, however, that in certain sentences a *NP* following a preposition which immediately follows the verb may passivize, as in 'This bed was slept in by George Washington'. A *NP* which does not immediately follow the verb (with perhaps an optional preposition intervening) never passivizes. From 'John presented a book to Bill' we do not get *'Bill was presented a book to'; nor do we have *'A book was presented Bill by John' as a passive of 'John presented Bill a book'. As a rough approximation, we may say that the passive relation holds between sentences of the form *NP V (P) NP X* and *NP be Ved (P) by NP X*, where V = verb, P = preposition, X is a variable indicating that anything may follow the second *NP*, and ( ) around P indicate that its presence is optional. In the passive form, the object of the active appears as subject of the passive, while the subject of the active shows up in a *by*-phrase in the passive.

Let us now see if it is possible to establish that one member of an active-passive pair is more basic in some sense. First, although there are certain sentences of the active form to which no passive corresponds, there are no passives without corresponding actives. Thus, although we have 'This tome weighs three pounds' but no *'Three pounds are weighed by this tome', there are no passives like 'She was screened by the CIA' without a corresponding active 'The CIA screened her'. The only exception to this last claim is presented by sentences like 'They are $\left\{\dfrac{\text{known}}{\text{said}}\right\}$ by everyone to be tapeworms', for which the active is at best strange: 'Everyone $\left\{\dfrac{\text{knows}}{\text{says}}\right\}$ them to be tapeworms'. However, there is an explanation of this phenomenon, based on the interaction of several transformations, which will be discussed at a later point.

Second, as noticed earlier, certain *NP*'s appear in subject position only as the passive member of an active-passive pair. However, there are no *NP*'s which ordinarily cannot appear in subject position in actives, but which may do so only if they appear in the *by*-phrase of a passive. Stating the distribution of such special *NP* subjects of passives as 'tabs' and 'a good deal' is simplified if we state in terms of their appearance as objects of actives. In this sense, again, actives turn out to be more basic.

Let us review the progress of this discussion of transformations. We have discovered that certain sentences of English bear to each other a special relation generally not obtaining between arbitrary pairs of sentences of the language. Sentences entering into such relationships are synonymous, or nearly so. Further, they bear quite definite syntactic relationships to each other, such as that between the syntactic form of the active and corresponding passive cited above. Finally, among the pairs that enter into the special relationships, which we might call *transformational relationships*, one member of each pair is more basic. Therefore, these relationships are assymetrical, in the sense that the pairs which enter into the relationship do so in a certain fixed order.

Roughly, then, a transformation is a relation between certain sentences of the language. The statement of this relationship is formulated in terms of the structural configurations of the sentences which characteristically enter into the relation in question. Thus, we might state the active-passive relation in terms of the ordered pair $(NP_1 V (P) NP_2 X, NP_2 be Ved (P) by NP_1 X)$, where the first member gives the structure of the more basic sentence, the active, and the second the structure of the less basic sentence, the passive. Another notation for this might be $NP_1 V (P) NP_2 X \Rightarrow NP_2 be Ved (P) by NP_1 X$. Here the statement of the transformational relation takes on the garb of a rewrite rule, but of a sort quite different from the phrase structure rules discussed above. Whereas phrase structure rules allow for the replacement of a single symbol by a string of symbols, rules of the above form, which we might call *transformational rules*, provide for the alteration of one tree configuration into another. Thus, in particular, the active-passive relation, which we shall call the *Passive Transformation*, effects changing a tree like (i) into one like (ii).

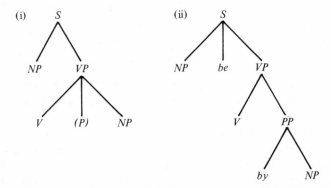

We might further change the notation for the *Passive* by labeling the constituents of the active form of the sentence to which the transformation applies, and then showing in the rewrite of the rule how these are rearranged in the *Passive*. In this notation we would write the *Passive* as follows:

$$NP \quad V \quad (P) \quad NP \quad X$$
$$1 \quad 2 \quad 3 \quad 4 \quad 5 \Rightarrow 4 \, be \, 2 \quad 3 \, by + 1 \quad 5$$

This is the notation commonly employed in works on transformational grammar. It will be discussed in detail in following sections.

Let us now introduce a new terminology for talking about transformational relations. We will say that a transformation *applies* to a sentence in tree form (the *input* to the transformation) to yield the second sentence of the transformationally related pair. We will call this second sentence the *derived* sentence.

The next logical question is whether transformations can apply to the output of transformations. That is, if transformations map sentences into sentences, then could not the output of one transformation form the input to another transformation? The answer is yes. Let us consider an example, taking passive as one of the transformations involved.

There is a transformation in English called *Subject-Verb Inversion* that forms questions; this transformation relates sentences such as 'It was snowing' and 'Was it snowing?' While it is beyond the scope of this discussion to go into the details of this transformation, the effects of its operation in cases such as the above are determinate and easily stated. In particular, if some form of the verb *be* immediately follows the subject, then the transformation moves it to the initial position. Notice now that the *Passive* transformation introduces the verb *be*. If *Subject-Verb Inversion* is to apply, it must wait until after *Passive* in order to place the *be* introduced by *Passive* in initial position. Thus, from an active sentence like 'George sees the goldfish', *Passive* applies first to generate 'The goldfish is seen by George', and finally *Subject-Verb Inversion* applies to yield 'Is the goldfish seen by George?'

Although many details have been omitted from this discussion, it is clear that transformations may apply to the output of other transformations, in the same way that phrase structure rules may apply to the output of phrase structure rules, i.e., may expand symbols themselves introduced by application of a previous rule. We may speak of a transformational derivation just as we spoke of derivations in phrase structure grammars. In phrase structure derivations, any rule of the grammar could apply at any point in the derivation. Examples such as the one above concerning the interaction of *Passive* and *Subject-Verb Inversion* indicate, however, that transformations must be extrinsically ordered in the grammar. That is, transformations must be listed in the grammar in a certain order, and derivations must be constrained such that a transformation is eligible to apply to a sentence only when its turn on the list is reached. The question of the conventions for ordering transformations will be discussed in greater detail later.

Derivations in a phrase structure grammar begin with an initial symbol, which forms the first line of the derivation. It is natural at this point to inquire into the nature of starting points for transformational derivations. This is best seen by working backwards, so to speak. Every sentence of English is the product of a transformational derivation. For expository purposes, we have spoken of transformations as though they were relations between actual sentences of English. In fact, transformational relations are more abstractly considered to be relations between two tree structures, neither of which need be actual sentences. For example, although we have spoken of the *Passive* as a relation between *sentences* like 'John saw Merry' and 'Merry was seen by John', in fact it is a relation between two underlying trees, one of which leads by the application of various other transformations to the active form, and the other to the passive form.

The output of transformational derivations are called *surface structures*. When we take a surface structure and "undo" the transformations involved in its derivation one at a time in reverse order from that in which they applied in the derivation, we arrive at something called *deep structure*. Deep structure has various interesting properties.

Although we *define* deep structure here to be that point at which transformational derivations begin, there is no reason to expect a priori that the deep structures of two surface structures will have any properties in common. In fact, however, when we take two arbitrary surface structures, each of which evidences very different processes of grammatical construction, such as 'What Tom ate was a pumpkin' and 'Was there thought to be a unicorn in the garden?', and reverse the transformations which apply to derive each surface structure, we arrive at two deep structures which share certain properties. There are two properties which all linguists agree are properties of deep structure: (1) deep structure determines a large part, if not all, of the meaning of the sentence; (2) the set of deep structures of a natural language are generable by a context free phrase structure grammar. Just how these properties are established will in part be the topic of later discussion. Given property (2), however, it is clear that the initial strings of transformational derivations are the trees generated by a *CF* grammar.

We have thus outlined two major aspects of the generation of sentences of natural language. Part of this generation consists of a derivation in a *CF* phrase structure grammar from the initial symbol *S*. To the output of this derivation are applied transformations, operations which change trees (bracketed terminal strings) into other trees. The transformations are applied subject to certain conventions, to be detailed below, one of which is that their application occurs in some fixed order. Thus, there is a natural division in the generation of sentences between the generation of a deep structure by the phrase structure rules, and the mapping of that deep structure into a surface structure by transformations. Corresponding to this division in processes, we speak of a *base component* of a grammar and a *transformational component*. The base component contains a phrase structure grammar and, according to Chomsky's (1965) theory, various processes concerning the insertion of lexical items into phrase structure trees. The transformational component contains a linearly ordered list of transformations. In this theory there were two more components to a full grammar of a natural language. The *phonological component* contains those rules necessary to map surface structures into a notation representing strings of sounds actually spoken, and the *semantic component* contains projection rules to map syntactic deep structures into semantic representations. We will have nothing further to say about phonology here, but later discussion will be devoted to the question of the existence and internal construction of the semantic component.

The concern of this chapter will be the specification in detail of the theory of transformations employed by grammarians at the time of Chomsky's publication of *Aspects of the Theory of Syntax* (1965). This theory derived historically from Chomsky (1955), and underwent modification only in detail during the succeeding ten years.

Formally described, a transformation of natural language is an ordered pair, the first member of which is a structural description (*SD*), and the second member of which is a structural change (*SC*). Informally, the *SD* specifies which trees the transformation applies to, and the *SC* specifies how these trees are changed by the operation of the transformation.

The theory of transformations is the theory of how transformations are constructed, and of the conventions which govern their application in transformational derivations in natural language. In particular, this theory must specify the construction of *SD*'s and the construction of *SC*'s, characteristic of transformations in natural language. Empirical issues are raised at each stage, and in many cases the question must be decided somewhat arbitrarily due to the lack of immediately relevant empirical data. Frequently, evidence bearing on particular decisions is totally lacking, and the viability of the decision can be determined only with reference to the viability and explanatory power of the total system to which the decision contributes.

We will now take up in turn the questions of the specification of *SD*'s, *SC*'s, and conventions governing the application of transformations.

3.2

Structural Descriptions

The SD of a transformation defines the set of tree structures to which that transformation applies. That such a restriction is necessary, i.e., that transformations do not apply to all possible tree structures of a language, can be seen by considering a few simple examples.

There is a transformation in English, called *Dative Movement*, which maps a sentence like (1a) into (1b).

(1)   a. *Alfred sent a letter to the girl.*
      b. *Alfred sent the girl a letter.*

If this transformation is applied to (2a), where 'to the moon' is interpreted as indicating a direction, then the ungrammatical sentence (2b) would be generated.

(2) a. *The Russians sent a machine to the moon.*
     b. **The Russians sent the moon a machine.*

Thus, some restriction on the transformation must allow it to apply to (1a) while preventing it from applying to (2a), otherwise the transformation would not correctly represent the linguistic competence of the native speaker of English. Such a restriction will be built into the *SD* of *Dative Movement*. If this restriction took the form of requiring the *NP* moved by the transformation to be in the dative case, then the theory of universal grammar would have to allow for transformations to mention the case of *NP*'s to which they apply. It is possible to see in such a case the interaction of considerations particular to a language and considerations of universal grammar.

The *Passive* transformation provides a second example indicating the necessity for restrictions on the application of transformations. As discussed above, this transformation maps (3a) into (3b), but must be prevented from changing (4a) into the ungrammatical (4b):

(3) a. *Urman ate meat.*
     b. *Meat was eaten by Urman.*

(4) a. *Urman ate last year.*
     b. **Last year was eaten by Urman.*

Again, the operation of the transformation must be limited to those trees specified by its *SD*. In this case, (4b) may be blocked by specifying that *Passive* applies only to noun phrases (*NP*) and not to adverbs (*Adv*) which follow a verb.

Crucial to defining *SD*'s formally in the standard theory is the notion of factorization of a tree. For trees generated by the phrase structure base of a transformational grammar, the definition of factorization is based on the definition of a derivation in such a grammar. Namely, if *f* is a line in a possible derivation of a tree by the phrase structure grammar, then *f* is a *factorization* of that tree. For example, consider the possible derivations of a tree like (5a) by the phrase structure rules for English.

(5) (a)

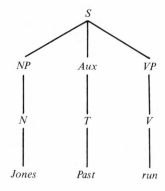

(b) *S*			(c) *S*			(d) *S*		
NP	*Aux*	*VP*	*NP*	*Aux*	*VP*	*NP*	*Aux*	*VP*
N	*Aux*	*VP*	*N*	*Aux*	*VP*	*NP*	*T*	*VP*
N	*T*	*VP*	*N*	*Aux*	*V*	*N*	*T*	*VP*
N	*T*	*V*	*N*	*T*	*V*	*N*	*T*	*V*

(e) *S*			(f) *S*			(g) *S*		
NP	*Aux*	*VP*	*NP*	*Aux*	*VP*	*NP*	*Aux*	*VP*
NP	*T*	*VP*	*NP*	*Aux*	*V*	*NP*	*Aux*	*V*
NP	*T*	*V*	*N*	*Aux*	*V*	*NP*	*T*	*V*
N	*T*	*V*	*N*	*T*	*V*	*N*	*T*	*V*

Each of the partial derivations listed above may be completed in any one of nine different ways. Thus, *N* could be expanded as 'Jones' first, and then *T* and finally *V* expanded, or then *V* and finally *T* expanded. Similarly, *T* could be expanded first as 'PAST', with the expansion of *V* and *N* coming in either order. Finally, *V* could be rewritten as 'run' first, with *T* and *N* coming in either order. In all, there are 54 different derivations of (5a). By definition, each line of each derivation is a factorization of (5a). Note that there are not 54 derivations times three lines per derivation different factorizations, since some lines occur in more than one derivation. For example, the lines *S*, *NP Aux VP*, and *NTV* occur in all derivations.

A simple rule of thumb for determining the factorizations of a tree consists in drawing lines horizontally through the tree such that each line at no point crosses a line connecting the nodes of the tree. The sequence of nodes through which each such horizontal line passes is a factorization of the tree. A few such lines are drawn through tree (5a) for illustration below.

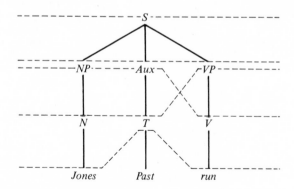

It will be necessary to consider factorizations of trees which are themselves the products of the operation of transformations. (Such trees are known as *derived structures*.) In such cases, we cannot rely on derivations in the phrase structure rules of the base component to define factorizations. However, it would be possible to write a new phrase structure grammar to generate each derived tree, in which case the definition given above will apply, since a factorization of such a derived tree will be any line of any derivation of the derived structure in the phrase structure grammar generating that tree. In practice, the technique of drawing horizontal lines, either mentally or with pencil and paper, may be employed in determining whether some sequence of symbols is a possible factorization of a tree.

It is possible now to define the notion of domination. If a labeled bracketing has two possible factorizations, $X\ A\ Y$ and $X\ W\ Y$, where X, Y, W are arbitrary strings in V^*, A is a single nonterminal, and A is higher on the tree than W, then A *dominates* W. If A dominates W, we write $A > W$. If A dominates W and for no B is it the case that $A > B$ and $B > W$, then A is the *lowest dominating node* of W.

This notion of domination concerns nodes and substrings dominated by nodes. In a slightly different version of this notion, we speak of nodes dominating nodes. Specifically, if $A > W$, and $B > Z$, where Z is some substring of W, then sometimes it is said that A dominates B. If A dominates B in the second sense, i.e., in the sense that if one proceeds "upwards" in the tree from node B, then eventually one reaches node A, and if no node intervenes between A and B, then we say that A *immediately dominates* B; the notation for this case would be $A \gg B$. The two slightly different notions of domination may be used interchangeably without confusion, and the notation for each is the same. In particular, if A is the lowest dominating node of W, then by analogy we may write $A \gg W$.

The general procedure behind constructing the SD of a transformation is to specify the trees to which this transformation applies by giving the factorizations of these trees. Roughly, a transformation applies to those trees which can be factored in certain ways, although more complicated conditions are also sometimes needed. For example, the transformation of *Dative Movement* discussed above applies to trees which can be factored $NP\ V\ NP\ NP$, where the second NP is marked [+ Dative]. It will be noticed immediately that this transformation applies to other trees which cannot be so factored, such as the tree underlying 'George gave a book to Harriet in the park'. Rather than specifying all the different possibilities for phrases following the two NP's by list, however, they are simply allowed by placing a variable in the SD of *Dative Movement*. Likewise, various different configurations occurring before the verb are allowed by placing a variable in front of V. Thus, the correct form of the SD of *Dative Movement* in part has the shape of the factorization $X\ V\ NP\ NP\ Y$, where X and Y are variables over terminal strings.

Trees subject to the *Passive* transformation must also be factorable as $NP\ V\ (P)\ NP\ X$, in addition to meeting certain other conditions. Further, it is possible that the trees to which some transformations apply meet conditions imposed by two factorizations, i.e., that such trees be factorable in two (or more) specified ways For example, the rule of *Extraposition* that maps (6a) into (6b) requires that the extraposed sentence be dominated by a *NP*.

(6)   a. *That horses sweat surprises no one.*
    b. *It surprises no one that horses sweat.*

This transformation applies to trees factorable as $X\ S\ Y$, where the S node is immediately dominated by a *NP*, i.e., where the tree is also factorable as $X\ NP\ Y$. This is usually written $X\ [S]_{NP}\ Y$, meaning that not only is the string factorable as $X\ S\ Y$ and $X\ NP\ Y$, but also that the NP of the second factorization dominates the S of the first.

With these examples in mind, it is possible to define more formally the notion "structural description of a transformation of natural language." Let us associate with each transformation a restricting class, Q, consisting of a finite set of factorizations, each of which has r terms for some fixed r. (By adding the null string as a term of a factorization, it is possible to guarantee that all factorizations have the same number of terms.) Thus, Q will have n factorizations $W_1^k, \ldots, W_r^k$ $(1 \leq k \leq n)$, each with r terms; Q may be defined to be the *structural description* of a transformation. A *proper analysis* with respect to Q of some terminal string, Z, with associated bracketing, K, will be a factorization of Z into an r-termed sequence, $Z_1, \ldots, Z_r$, where each Z_i is dominated by the node W_i in K, such that the sequence $(W_1, \ldots W_r)$ is an element of Q.

A Boolean condition on analyzability (Chomsky, 1965, Chap. 3) is a Boolean condition on how a P-marker is to be analyzed in terms of the elements in Q. Before discussing this in more detail, it is relevant to make precise the notion of Boolean condition. In general, any combination of elements by the truth functional connectives & (and), v (or), and − (not) is a Boolean combination. A non-Boolean combination would involve use of essentially more powerful devices, such as quantifiers from the first order predicate calculus.

The following example will illustrate the application of this terminology. As discussed above, the *Passive* transformation in English fronts not only *NP*'s which immediately follow a transitive verb, but also certain *NP*'s which are the objects of prepositional phrases, under conditions not fully understood. *Passive* can map the structure underlying (7a) into (7b).

(7)   a. *George Washington slept in this bed.*
    b. *This bed was slept in by George Washington.*

Thus, *Passive* applies not only to trees which are factored $X\ NP\ V\ \varnothing\ NP\ Y$, but also to trees factored $X\ NP\ V\ P\ NP\ Y$. These two parsings would be disjunctive conditions on analyzability—that is, a tree must satisfy either one or the other factorization (plus further conditions) in order for *Passive* to apply. Notice the symbol for the null string, $\varnothing$, is inserted to guarantee that both factorizations have the same number of terms. The notation commonly employed in cases such as the above, in which a rule involves two strings of symbols, one of which is a subpart of the other, is called the *parenthesis notation*. The two disjunctive environments listed above would be collapsed by this notation as $X\ NP\ V\ (P)\ NP\ Y$. A convention associated with this notation prescribes that the rule applies in the longer environment first if possible, and only if that fails may it apply in the shorter environment. Although this convention has no empirical consequences as regards application of the *Passive*, it does play an important role in the construction of phonological rules.

If the conditions on analyzability are extended beyond strictly Boolean conditions, then membership in the class of transformational grammars so defined is correspondingly increased. Such extension would represent a weakening of the explanatory power of the theory of universal grammar of which the above definition of "structural description" is a part.

In stating *SD*'s, it is possible to place additional conditions of two sorts on terms of factorizations in Q. First, it is possible to require that two terms of a certain factorization be identical. For example, in *Reflexivization*, one *NP* is marked as reflexive if it is identical to a *NP* which precedes it in a simple sentence. Thus, this rule would map an underlying structure like (8a), but not (8b), into (8c).

(8) a. *Mitsie saw Mitsie in the mirror.*
     b. *Mitsie saw Michael in the mirror.*
     c. *Mitsie saw herself in the mirror.*

The *SD* of *Reflexivization* would contain the factorization $X\ NP\ Y\ NP\ Z$, where application of the rule would be contingent on term two of this factorization being equal to term four (in addition to the condition mentioned above, that both *NP*'s be within the same simple sentence).

The definition of the notion of identity must be specified by the theory of universal grammar. Chomsky (1965) argues that this definition must include intended identity of reference. For example, (8a) would not be reflexivized to (8c) if the speaker was refering to two different people, each having the name 'Mitsie'. The notation Chomsky suggests for representing intended identity of reference consists in affixing indices to the *NP*'s, with identical indices representing identity of reference. The particular integer chosen as an index being irrelevant, the usual practice is to affix variables over integers, and the identity of variables indicates identity of indices. Under this convention, the case of (8a), which reflexivizes, would be written as (9a), and the case that does not as (9b).

(9) a. *Mitsie$_i$ saw Mitsie$_i$ in the mirror.*
     b. *Mitsie$_i$ saw Mitsie$_j$ in the mirror.*

The second kind of restriction possible for terms of factorizations in structural descriptions consists in requiring identity of some term(s) with one of a fixed, finite list of terminal strings. For example, one instance of the rule of *Subject-Verb Inversion* in English permutes the string 'Tense *have*' with the subject (mapping the structure underlying 'George has failed' into the structure underlying 'Has George failed?'). In stating this case of the *Inversion* transformation formally, it is required that a certain term of a factorization be identical with a terminal string of one symbol, '*have*'.

This completes the sketch of the formal construction of *SD*'s. The discussion can be summarized in the following definition: A *structural description* of a transformation is a class of factorizations, Q, each with r terms for some fixed r, and some Boolean condition stating how trees are to be analyzed in terms of the members of Q. It is possible for two terms of a factorization in Q to be required to be identical, or for a term to be required to be identical to one of a finite list of terminal strings, fixed for the grammar.

EXERCISES FOR SECTION 3.2

1. The sentence, 'Flying planes can be dangerous', is structurally ambiguous (represented by two different trees) on surface structure. Write each surface structure tree, and list three factorizations for which the trees are different, and three for which they are the same.

2. In a hitherto undiscovered language, Mayspeak, the transformation *Breaking* applies to trees which have an analysis *NP NP egg V S* or *PP AP S ∅ V*, except when the first three constituents of the first or the second and third constituents of the second are dominated by the node Z. Write the *SD* for this transformation as a Boolean condition on factorizations in a restricting class, Q.

3.3

Structural Changes

The *SC* of a transformation defines how that transformation operates on those trees that meet the *SD* of the transformation. The possible *SC*'s that a transformation of natural language may perform on trees is specified formally in terms of three different elementary structural changes, also known as the *elementary transformations*. The elementary transformations are as follows:

1. *The Deletion Elementary:* This elementary transformation has the effect of deleting the ith term of an r-termed factorization of a tree. Let us employ the notation D_i^r for the elementary transformation that deletes the ith term. Given the factorization of a tree into the terms $W_1, \ldots W_i, \ldots W_r$, we define $D_1^r (W_1, \ldots W_i, \ldots W_r)$ to be $W_1, \ldots \varnothing \ldots W_r$, where $\varnothing$ is the symbol for the null string, mentioned above.

For example, at an intermediate stage in the formation of relative clauses, a sentence like (10a) has the representation given in (10b).

(10)   a. *The book which George wrote was about fantasies of fairies.*
       b. *The book which book George wrote was about fantasies of fairies.*

A transformation maps (10b) into a structure which eventuates as (10a), by deleting the repeated head of the relative clause, 'book'. The part of this transformation which is of interest here applies to trees factorable as '$X\ NP\ wh\ NP\ Y$' (where *wh* is a morpheme which is common to such words as 'what', 'where', 'why', and 'how'). This transformation deletes the second of the two NP's, providing that the NP's are identical. The structural change of this transformation would contain the elementary transformation D_4^5. The notation commonly used for writing such a deletion operation is to label the terms with consecutive integers, replacing the deleted term with a $\varnothing$ in the rewrite of the transformation. Thus, the transformation discussed above might be written as (11).

(11) X NP wh NP Y

       1   2   3   4   5 $\Rightarrow$

       1   2   3 $\varnothing$ 5   condition: $2 = 4$

The derived constituent structure (*DCS*) resulting from application of the deletion elementary is easily specified. The node deleted and the substring it dominates are excised from the tree. If the deleted node is exhaustively dominated by another node, then this node will dominate nothing and will disappear by convention. If the result of a deletion is to leave in the tree a node that does not branch, then this node will disappear at a certain point in the derivation by a convention known as *Tree Pruning* (see Ross, 1967, for a discussion of this convention).

2. *The Substitution Elementary:* The substitution elementary effects the substitution of the jth through kth factors of a SD for the ith factor. Where

the factorizations in the SD under consideration have r terms each, we would use the notation $S_{i,j-k}^r$. In the case in which the substitution replaces the ith term by only one other term, i.e., in which $j = k$, we write $S_{i,j}^r$.

For example, in an analysis of the *Passive* transformation in English held at one time by many linguists, the NP in object position was substituted for the subject NP, while the subject NP was substituted for a passive marker, *Pass* in the VP. Thus, by the operation of *Passive* in this analysis, a string like (12a) would be transformed into (12b).

(12) a. NP_1 *Aux V* NP_2 *by Pass*

      b. NP_2 *Aux V   by* NP_1

In this analysis, the passive morpheme, *be* $+$ *en*, is inserted into rightmost position in the *Aux*, although we need not be concerned with this aspect of *Passive* here. The version of the *Passive* which transforms (12a) into (12b) would make two uses of the substitution elementary; the first term of the SD is substituted for the sixth term of the factorization, and the fourth term is substituted for the first term. This transformation employs the particular elementaries denoted by $S_{6,1}^6$ and $S_{1,4}^6$. The notation for such substitutions common in the literature is indicated in (13).

(13) *NP Aux V NP by Pass*

      1   2   3   4   5   6 $\Rightarrow$

      4   2   3 $\varnothing$ 5   1

3. *The Adjunction Elementary:* The adjunction elementary operates to adjoin the jth through the kth terms of a SD to the right or the left of the ith term of a SD. We may denote the adjunction elementary by $AR_{i,j-k}^r$ and $AL_{i,j-k}^r$, depending on whether the adjunction is to the right or to the left. The adjunction effected by the adjunction elementary is commonly refered to as *sister adjunction*, and it is denoted by the symbol $+$. Adjoining the node B to the left of the node A in a configuration like that in (14a) yields a DCS in which B becomes immediately dominated by the node that immediately dominates A, as in (14b); adjoining B to the right of A in (14a) will yield (14c).

(14) (a)   (b)   (c)

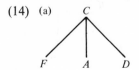
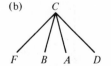
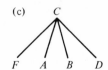

A common way of stating the *Dative* transformation in English involves use of the adjunction elementary. This transformation maps structures underlying sentences like (15a) into structures underlying (15b).

(15) a. *Dana sent a post card to her aunt Dwight.*
      b. *Dana sent her aunt Dwight a post card.*

Schematically, *dative* maps a string like (16a) into (16b).

(16) a. $NP \ V \ NP_1 \ to \ NP_2$

      b. $NP \ V \ NP_2 \ NP_1 \ \varnothing$

In this case, NP_2 is adjoined to NP_1 on the left. Thus, NP_2 is immediately dominated by VP in DCS, as VP immediately dominates NP_1. In particular, the adjunction elementary employed in *Dative* is $AL^5_{3.5}$. Notice also that *Dative* written as above employs the deletion elementary D^5_4. Formally, the SC of *Dative* would be specified as: $AL^5_{3.5}$; D^5_4. The notation common in the literature is indicated in (17).

(17) $NP \quad V \quad NP \quad to \quad NP$

      1   2   3   4   5 $\Rightarrow$

      1   2   5 + 3 $\varnothing$

A particular species of adjunction is known as Chomsky-adjunction. Described informally, if a node B is Chomsky-adjoined to a node A, then a copy of A is built over A which then immediately dominates both A and B. Thus, (18b, c) result from (18a) by Chomsky-adjoining B to the right and left of A, respectively.

(18) (a)   (b)   (c)

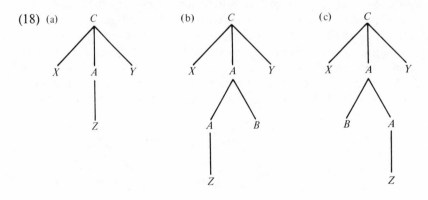

The operation of Chomsky-adjunction is employed frequently in the analysis of natural language. We may choose the transformation called *Appositive Clause Swooping* as an example. This transformation forms appositive clauses from deep structure conjunction, mapping a structure like (19a) into (19b).

(19)   (a)

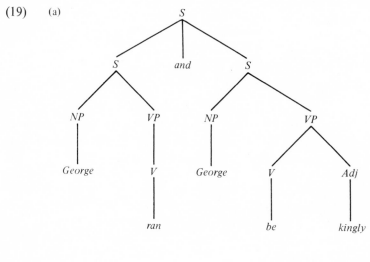

(b)

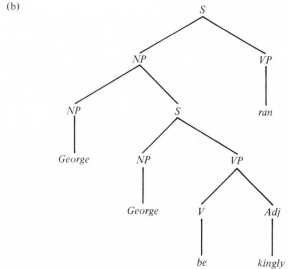

Sentence (19b) would appear as 'George, who was kingly, ran' on surface structure. In the application of *Swooping* to (19a), the second conjunct is Chomsky-adjoined to the *NP* in subject position of the first conjunction.

Chomsky-adjunction is frequently discussed as though it were a new elementary transformation, distinct from the adjunction elementary commonly known as sister adjunction. However, if trees are defined as equivalence classes of derivations, as discussed in Chapter One, then it is possible to construct Chomsky-adjunction in such a way that it becomes an instance of sister adjunction. Suppose we define the derivations indicated by (20a, b, c) to be all in the same equivalence class, i.e., to define the same tree, (20d).

(20) (a) $X\ A\ Y$ (b) $X\ A\ Y$ (c) $X\ A\ Y$

        $X\ Z\ Y$ $X\ A\ e\ Y$ $X\ e\ A\ Y$

                     $X\ Z\ e\ Y$ $X\ e\ Z\ Y$

(d) $X\ A\ Y$ (where e is the null symbol)
$\quad\quad\ |$
$\quad\quad Z$

Then, if we define the node B to be sister adjoined to the right of A in the second line of (20b), replacing e, the result will be the tree (21a).

(21)   (a) X A Y (b) X A Y

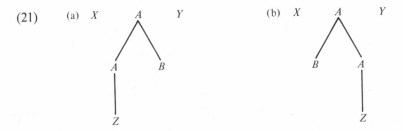

Allowing B to replace e in sister adjunction to the left of A in the second line of (20c) results in tree (21b), under the normal procedures for defining trees in terms of equivalence classes of derivations.

If we think of the tree (20d) as being changed into either (21a) or (21b) by Chomsky-adjunction, it looks as though a new copy of node A is produced from nowhere. Thus it seems as though Chomsky-adjunction must be defined as a new elementary transformation of adjunction. However, if we treat trees as equivalence classes of derivations, where transformational operations defined on trees are thus defined on the corresponding sets of derivations, then Chomsky-adjunction may be formally described as sister adjunction.

The usual notation for indicating Chomsky-adjunction is the $\#$ symbol. The formal description of the *Relative Clause Swooping* transformation mentioned above, written in the notation now common in the literature of linguistics, would appear as (22).

(22) $[X \ NP \ X]_S$ and $[X \ NP \ X]_S$

   1 2 3   4 5 6 7 $\Rightarrow$

   1 2 $\#[(4) \ 5 \ 6 \ 7]_S$ 3   condition: $2 = 6$
          $[+Wh]$

(The $[+wh]$ morpheme on the swooped relative clause is the origin of the *wh*-word in the appositive clause after the transformation of *Relative Clause Formation* applies. If the conjunction is carried along [term 4], the resulting surface structure would appear like 'George, and he is kingly, ran'.)

This completes the description of the elementary transformations. The structural change of a transformation is simply a list of elementary transformations which operate on the tree when that transformation applies. The notation common among linguists does not involve specific listing of the elementary transformations operative in the *SC* of particular transformations, but these are reconstructible from the usual notation, as exemplified above.

Proposed changes in the Standard Theory frequently involve changes in the list of possible elementary transformations. Some of these changes would involve adding a new elementary, in which case the generative capacity of the class of grammars defined under the proposal may be greater than that of those defined under the original theory. (As outlined in Chapter Four, an increase in generative capacity entails a corresponding net decrease in explanatory power.) For example, it has been proposed that the elementary operation known alternatively as *inversion* or *flip* be added to the three mentioned above. This operation would interchange the position of two terms of a *SD*, where the two terms in their new positions are dominated by the lowest node dominating both of them in their original positions. The postulated elementary would figure in such transformations as *Passive*, replacing the analysis which involves two uses of the substitution elementary.

Other proposed changes in the list of elementaries involve removing some elementary, such as the deletion elementary. Such proposals make it necessary to reanalyze those transformations in which the elementary to be eliminated played a part. Removing an elementary would in some cases reduce the generative capacity of the class of transformational grammars, resulting in grammars with less rich devices of formal description, and thus with greater explanatory power. This reduction in formal apparatus must in all cases, however, result in grammars that meet the minimal condition of descriptive adequacy—ability to generate correctly the sentences of a natural language.

3.4

The Condition on
Recoverability of Deletions

A theory of grammar which allows the SC of a transformation to be any arbitrary collection of elementary transformations is much too rich, in the sense of counting as a possible grammatical transformation an operation which deletes, say, all of the terms of its SD. Such an operation could be found in no natural language, and it is a deficiency of the theory outlined above not to exclude in some principled way such extreme cases.

The condition on recoverability of deletions is an attempt to constrain this theory of SC's by restricting the set of elementary transformations which may be found in the SC of any particular transformation. The condition on recoverability requires that if some term of a SD is deleted or substituted for in the course of a transformational operation, then that term must either be identical to some term not deleted by that transformation, or identical to one of a finite list of terms fixed for the grammar.

Let us consider first a case in which the term deleted is identical to some other nondeleted term of the SD. English contains a transformation called *Equi NP Deletion* which deletes the subject of an embedded sentence under identity to a *NP* in the next higher sentence, subject to certain restrictions that need not be of concern here. This transformation will map (23a) into (23b).

(23) a. *For John to join the army would frighten John.*
      b. *To join the army would frighten John.*

(A transformation of *Complementizer Deletion* follows *Equi NP Deletion*, eliminating the 'for' from [23a].)

The subcase of *Equi NP Deletion* that applies to (23a) might be written as (24).

(24) [for NP X]$_S$ V NP

  1   2   3   4   5 $\Rightarrow$

  1    $\emptyset$ 3   4   5   condition: $2 = 5$

This transformation meets the condition on recoverability of deletions, because the term deleted on any application of the transformation will be identical to some term not deleted by that application of the transformation. The term that remains may be deleted by a later application of some transformation, but this would not constitute a violation of the condition on recoverability, so long as the subsequent deletion proceeds under identity to a term which remains. For example, sentence (25c) is derived from (25a) by two applications of *Equi NP Deletion*, the second of which deletes the term which remained undeleted in the first application.

(25) a. *John wanted for John to be able for John to run.*
      b. *John wanted for John to be able to run.*
      c. *John wanted to be able to run.*

The transformation which deletes 'for' in certain environments does not perform the deletion under identity to another 'for', but the transformation does not violate the condition on recoverability, since 'for' is placed as a member of the fixed finite list of terms. This list contains those lexical and grammatical formatives which can be deleted without identity to other remaining identical formatives. Another example is provided by the deletion of indefinites in English. The transformation called *Indefinite Deletion* effects this deletion; it maps (26a) into (26b) and (27a) into (27b).

(26) a. *George ate something.*
      b. *George ate.*

(27) a. *George was seen by someone.*
      b. *George was seen.*

In these cases deletion proceeds without identity to some term that remains undeleted. However, the deleted term can be made identical to a grammatical formative marked indefinite in the finite list of deletables in English.

The condition on recoverability suggests by its name that, as formulated above, it permits reconstruction from surface structure of all terms deleted in the course of a transformational derivation. Thus, we can reconstruct the missing subjects in (25c) from the presence of the undeleted term, plus, perhaps, knowledge that *Equi NP Deletion* has applied in the transformational history of the sentence. The missing indefinites can be constructed from (26b) and (27b) given the knowledge of the environment for the application of *Indefinite Deletion*.

When the condition on recoverability was first formulated (Katz and Postal, 1964), it was claimed without proof (p. 80) that imposing this restriction on the class of potential grammars of natural languages renders each language generated fully recursive. (A language is *recursive* if, given some string over the vocabulary in which the sentences of the language are written, there is a computation procedure which will determine in a finite number of steps whether or not the string is in the language.) We want grammars of natural languages to generate only recursive languages. Other-wise the theory of grammar could say nothing stronger than that the grammar of a natural language is some computation device, without being able to place constraints on the form of that device. Such a theory would be at a loss to explain child language acquisition, for there would be no way to choose a device from the many that generated strings in agreement with the experienced linguistic data.

However, later work on various formalized models of transformational grammars (e.g., Kimball, 1967) has established that the condition on recoverability is not by itself sufficient to guarantee that languages generated by these devices are recursive. That is, transformational grammars have the full generative power of unrestricted rewrite systems (discussed in Chapter One). This fact demonstrates the need for further empirical work to constrain the generative capacity of transformational grammars.

3.5

Conventions for the Application of Transformations

This section will deal with various conventions governing the application of transformations. The specification of these conventions is a part of universal grammar; as such, their formulation relies on arguments that involve several levels of abstraction. Evidence for or against some proposed convention is thus frequently difficult to find. The difficulties lie not so much in the difficulty of surveying different languages to test for the presence of some convention, as in finding relevant evidence within even one language. One reason for the paucity of evidence concerning conventions is that no language learner needs access to data within his own language that provide justification for one or another convention, as he brings knowledge of the universal conventions for applications of transformations as part of the mental equipment with which he undertakes to learn a language. Thus, whereas the language learner must find evidence for the existence and formulation of some transformation particular to his language, the same is not true of those aspects of the structure of his language that are universal.

The central convention governing the application of transformations is the principle of the transformational cycle, usually known simply as the cycle. The transformations of a language are divided into those which apply according to this principle, called the *cyclic* transformations, and those that do not, called *last cyclic*, *precyclic*, and *anywhere* transformations. For the present, we will confine our attention to the cyclic transformations. The principle of the cycle is best illustrated by considering the interaction of two transformations on various sentences of a given deep structure. The transformations to be dealt with are *Passive* and *Subject Raising*. This latter transformation operates in part to raise the subject of an embedded sentence (subordinate clause) from that sentence into derived object position in the next sentence. It is illustrated by sentences like (27).

(27)

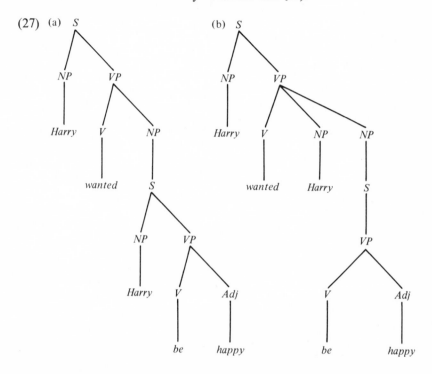

One final transformation called *Reflexivization* applies to (27b) to produce the surface structure, 'Harry wants himself to be happy'. *Reflexivization* changes the second 'Harry' to 'himself' under the influence of the identical subject 'Harry'.

Let us see how the principle of the cycle governs the application of *Subject Raising* and *Passive* to a deep structure with multiple embedded sentences. The principle states that cyclic transformations apply in a fixed order, in this case in the order mentioned above, first to the most deeply embedded sentence, and then to successively higher sentences, applying each transformation in turn where possible in its order to each sentence. Application of the list of transformations to the most deeply embedded sentence is called the *first cycle*; application to successively higher sentences constitutes the second, third, and so on, cycles. The cycle is best understood by example. In the following, *Subject Raising* (*SR*) fails to apply to the lowest sentence, but *Passive* does, yielding (28b) from (28a).

On cycle two, which occurs on the middle sentence, *SR* applies first,

(28)   (a)

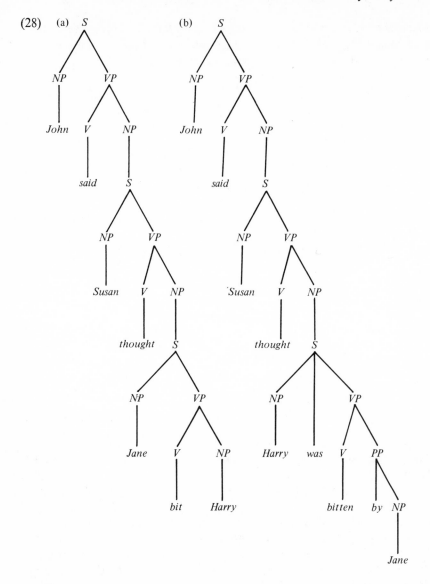

raising the derived subject of the embedded sentence, 'Harry', into object position. The word order does not change, but the constituent structure does. The result is (28c).

Details of the derivation, such as the appearance of 'to have been' under the *Aux* in the lowest sentence, are omitted here, as they are not directly relevant to the operation of the cycle in governing the interaction of *SR* and *Passive*. Next *Passive* applies on the second cycle to place 'Harry' again in derived subject position. The result is (28d).

(28) (c)

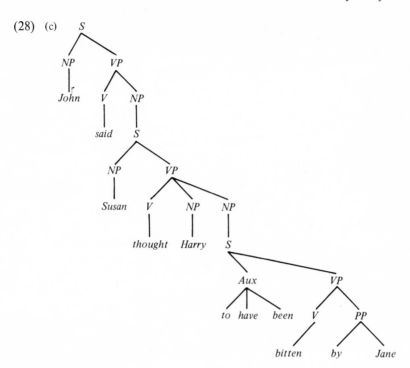

(28) (d)

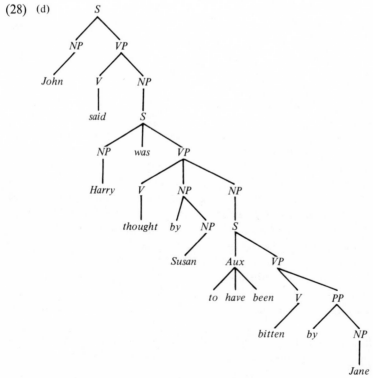

On the last cycle, in which *SR* and *Passive* apply on the topmost sentence, 'Harry' is again raised, and then passivized into subject position. The final tree is (28e).

(28) (e)

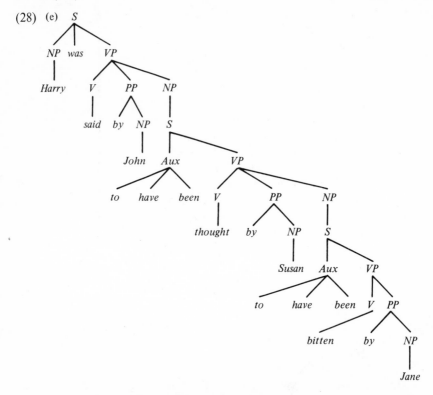

The reader will notice that from a deep structure like 'John said that Susan thought that Jane bit Harry', in which 'Harry' appears in object position in the most deeply embedded sentence, it was possible through the interaction of *SR* and *Passive* in application under the principle of the cycle to derive (28e), in which 'Harry' is the subject of the highest (matrix) sentence.

We can state the principle of the cycle more abstractly now: If $T_1, \ldots, T_k$ are the cyclic transformations of a grammar, then they apply in order, first to the most deeply embedded sentence of a deep structure, and then successively to higher sentences. In this way the linearly ordered list of transformations works up the tree until the last cycle on the topmost sentence. The transformations which are not cyclic apply on this topmost cycle interspersed in order among the application of the cyclic transformations on that cycle. These are thus called the *last cyclic* transformations. For example, the transformation which forms questions is a last cyclic transformation.

Besides cyclic and last cyclic transformations, there are arguments for the existence of transformations which apply under precyclic conventions to the whole deep structure before any cyclic transformation applies. An example of a precyclic transformation is *Sentence Pronominalization*, which maps (29a) into (29b).

(29) a. *Mafort believes that the world is flat, and Twagmore believes that the world is flat too.*
       b. *Mafort believes that the world is flat, and Twagmore believes it too.*

Sentence Pronominalization (*S-Pro*) changes the second occurrence of 'that the world is flat' into 'it' under identity with the preceding sentence. It is possible to see that *S-Pro* must apply before any cyclic transformation by considering sentences like (30).

(30) *Michelle was thought to be pregnant, although Sam wasn't eager to believe it.*

This sentence is derived from a deep structure like (31).

(31)

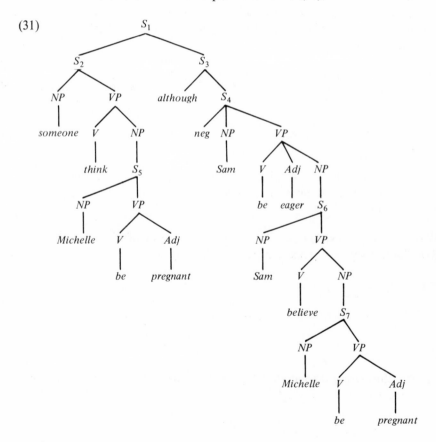

For *S-Pro* to change (31) into (30), S_7 must be pronominalized under identity to S_5. However, the lowest sentence which dominates both S_5 and S_7 is S_1. If *S-Pro* were cyclic, then by the time it could apply on the final cycle, S_5 would have been broken up by *Raising* and *Passive* on the S_2 cycle. The derived S_2 would be 'Michelle was thought to be pregnant' (a general deletion operation removes 'someone' from the passivized sentence). Thus, the conditions of identity between S_5 and S_7 would no longer hold on the S_1 cycle, since S_5 in particular would no longer exist as a sentence. It is argued on the basis of cases like these that a transformation like *S-Pro* must apply to the whole tree before any cyclic transformation applies. Once a transformation has applied in the precycle, it is no longer available at any later point in the derivation.

In addition to the conventions for cyclic, precyclic, and last cyclic application, there is a *convention of simultaneous application* (*CSA*). This convention requires that when a transformation applies to a tree, it applies at as many places in the tree as possible. That is, the tree is factored in as many ways as possible to fit the *SD* of the transformation, which then applies simultaneously in each subtree that meets the *SD*. An example of a transformation applying under this convention is provided by *Affix Hopping*, which permutes affixes around following verbals. This transformation would map (32a) into (32b).

(32)   a. *Tns M have+en be+ing run*
        b. *M #Tns have be #en run #ing* (*#* *being the sign for Chomsky-adjunction*)

The transformation is stated as in (33).

(33) *X Af v Y*
     1 2 3 4 $\Rightarrow$ 1 3 #2 4, where '*v*' stands for modals, 'have', 'be', and all verbs; and 'tns' (tense) 'en' (past participle), and 'ing' (present participle) are affixes.

We can break up a string like (32a) in three ways, each of which will meet the *SD* of *Affix Hopping*. This is indicated schematically in (34).

(34)   *Af   v   Af   v*

            Tns   M   have + en   be + ing   run

                                        Af   v

The transformation then applies to move each affix over the following verbal at the same time, under *CSA*.

IV

Constraints on
Grammars and
Generative Capacity

Preliminary Remarks

The theory of universal grammar must specify the form which the grammar of a possible natural language may take, and in addition it must specify an evaluation metric to rank possible grammars on some scale of complexity. Results of research on problems of universal grammar are stated in terms of contributions to further specification of the form of a possible grammar. In particular, results may take the form of constraining the generative capacity of the class of grammars proposed as models for the grammars of natural language.

The conception of the task of linguistics stated above, due to Chomsky, embodies certain hypotheses about the nature of language. It will be the purpose of this chapter to untangle the chain of reasoning which leads to the formulation of research problems in terms of placing constraints on classes of grammars, and to make explicit the hypothesis about the nature of language implicit in this way of thinking.

We begin by recapitulating some of the discussion of Chapter Two. Let us define the *generative capacity* of a class of grammars to be the set of languages generated by grammars in that class. For example, the generative capacity of the class of regular *(CF, CS)* grammars is the set of regular *(CF, CS)* languages. Given two classes of grammars, C_1 and C_2, the generative capacity of C_1 is said to be greater than that of C_2 if the set of languages generated by C_1 grammars properly includes the set of languages generated by C_2 grammars. Given two classes of grammars, C_i, C_j, it is not necessarily the case that the generative capacity of one is less than that of the other. That is, it will not always be true that the generative capacity of, say, C_i, is either less than, equal to, or greater than that of C_j. Compare the class of all regular grammars over a vocabulary, V, containing exactly four nonterminal symbols, versus the class of context free grammars which generate finite languages. There are an infinite number of different grammars in each class, but each class contains a language not generated by any grammar of the other class. For example, the language $a^n b^k$ (all n, k) is in the first class, but clearly not in the second, as it is an infinite language. The language consisting of exactly one string, *abcdef*, cannot be generated by a regular grammar containing exactly four nonterminals (although it may be contained in a larger language generated by such a grammar). We say the generative capacities of the first and second classes of grammar described above are *incomparable*. The generative capacities of C_i and C_j are incomparable if some language generated by a grammar in C_i is generated by no grammar in C_j, and conversely.

It is important to distinguish comparisons of weak versus strong generative capacities. For example, let C_1 be the class of all *CF* grammars, and let C_2 be the class of *CF* grammars which are *binary branching* (a grammar is binary branching if it contains only rules of the form $A \rightarrow X$, where X is a string of two or less than two symbols). It can be shown that any *CF* language can be generated by a binary branching *CF* grammar. Thus, C_1 and C_2 have the same weak generative capacity. However, C_1 and C_2 do not have the same strong generative capacity; C_1 has a greater strong generative capacity than C_2.

Let us consider, finally, the case in which both C_i and C_j contain exactly one grammar. If the language generated by the only grammar in C_i is the same as that generated by the only grammar in C_j, then these two classes have the same generative capacity. Otherwise they are incomparable with respect to generative capacity. Thus, the definitions put forth above do not allow easy comparison of complexity of particular grammars; they adapt most naturally only when the complexity of the grammars of different

acquired is underdetermined by the data in many respects, yet different individuals exposed to the same language (each through potentially different sets of linguistic experience) internalize grammars which, if not the same, are sufficiently similar to permit communication.

It is worthwhile to consider this matter in more detail by taking a concrete point of universal grammar as an example. Let us assume for the moment the null hypothesis, that the language learner brings with him no knowledge of the structure of natural language to the task of language learning, and examine what conclusions he would have to draw on the basis of what evidence in order to deduce the principle of the transformational cycle on the basis of observed sentences in English.

The first, and perhaps least trivial, task would be that of casting his syntactic experience in transformational terms. He would somehow have to recognize pairs of sentences with the same meaning as being related in a special way. Assuming the learner chose to perceive observed sentences as bearing the hierarchical structure of phrase structure organization (a matter by no means trivial; other types of organization, such as deriving statistical information from expected occurrence in left to right order, might seem initially more plausible), he would then have to work out some theory of the construction of transformations which would predict which sentences could be related transformationally. Remember that the data involved in these decisions is indirect, as transformations characteristically relate trees that appear as intermediate stages of derivation and show up on surface structure only after they have undergone further transformational alteration, sometimes quite far-reaching in nature.

Supposing now that our learner has deduced the existence of transformations, he next will need to make the observation that they apply in derivations in some fixed linear order. Of course, data relevant for determination of order frequently rely on the *nonoccurrence* or ungrammaticality of certain strings of words. He would never experience these in adult speech, and perhaps could expect to test some hypothesis concerning ordering only by uttering various sentences to see if they drew negative reaction. Of course, the reaction could be to the content of the sentences rather than their grammatical form; parents generally expect children to speak ungrammatical but understandable English up into their teens, and might be unlikely to correct grammatical mistakes consistently. (One can see here how hopeless would be a theory of learning which attempted to explain language acquisition on the basis of very meagre kinds of generalization from experience such as reinforced response to some stimulus.) The conclusion that transformations must be ordered in their application to simple sentences (sentences with no embeddings), and the determination of the correct order for English, would then have to be tested by the language learner for complex sentences, which are themselves made up of many sentences. In particular, to "discover" the cycle the learner might need to have experience of sentences like 'Harry was thought by Jane to have been said by Mike to have been kicked by Susan', whose likelihood of occurrence is, needless to say, slight.

Without the assumption of universal grammar, there is no guarantee that two speakers will go through this lengthy process to learn the principle of the transformational cycle; i.e., there is no guarantee that any two speakers will internalize the same grammar, which is contrary to the observed fact that speakers acquire grammars that are at least similar in many basic respects.

Considerations such as those adduced above lead to the conclusion that universal grammar exists, and that perhaps a large part of the structure of any natural language is a direct reflection of universal principles of organization of language that are part of the mental apparatus of all members of the species *homo sapiens.* The question of determining the exact form of the principles of universal grammar is empirical. We will outline one theory of universal grammar in the next section.

To explain language acquisition, then, the linguist must be able to specify the form of universal grammar, i.e., the form of the grammar of any human language, in sufficient detail to account for how the child draws the observed conclusions about the language from the data to which he is exposed. It is easy to see that the more constrained the generative capacity of the class of grammars proposed by universal grammar as models for grammars of natural language, the closer the linguist is to explaining language acquisition. As the generative capacity is decreased, the number of different grammars consistent with a given set of data among which the child must choose (by, say, implementation of a simplicity metric ranking grammars according to complexity) becomes more limited. The more constrained the generative capacity of a class of grammars, the more limited is the form of the languages generated by grammars of that class. If the language to which the child is exposed is of a form generated by only one grammar specified as a possible grammar by the theory of universal grammar, then the phenomenon of acquisition in that case is explained. If a number of possible grammars are compatible with the data, then the language learner must choose the right grammar in some principled way. The principles of choice in such a case are called the simplicity metric—an unfortunate term, as it suggests an appeal to some extralinguistic notion of simplicity.

Thus it is that advance in knowledge of linguistic universals in the above described view of linguistics consists of placing additional grammatical constraints on universal grammar. The more limited the generative capacity of the class of grammars available as potential grammars for human languages, the closer to an explanation of child language acquisition the linguist has come. Adding new mechanisms to grammar which increase the generative capacity of the resulting class of grammars is an overall loss in explanatory power of universal grammar, and each such addition must be justified by empirical considerations.

EXERCISES FOR SECTION 4.2

1. Consider the following condition on phrase structure grammars: If a rule applies at some stage of a derivation, then it must apply everywhere it can. Thus, for example, given a rule $B \rightarrow X$, and an intermediate string in the derivation, $YBWBZ$, then under the proposed condition the rule must apply to yield $YXWXZ$, i.e., it applies to all B's, and it cannot apply to yield just, say, $YBWXZ$, or $YXWBZ$. Does the proposed condition constrain the generative capacity (strong or weak) of the class of CF grammars?

2. Consider a class of grammars which contains grammars which can generate languages with the property that in some fixed spelling, the nth word of each sentence of the language has n letters (phonemes). For example, 'A ma was what Jones wanted' would be a sentence of such a language. Could the theory of this class of grammars be acceptable as the theory of universal grammar? Why?

3. Consider two different acquisition devices with the following properties: When fed the strings aa, bb, $abab$, $aabb$, the first device constructs a grammar which generates the following sorts of strings: $ababab$, $aaabbb$, $abababab$, $aaaabbbb$, . . . ; the second constructs a grammar which generates strings of the following sorts: $ababab$, $abababab$, $ababababab$, . . . , $aabbaa$, $aabbaabb$, $aabbaabbaa$, ... What hypothesis concerning the internal structure of these devices would explain their respective behavior?

4.3

The Standard Theory

We have outlined the necessity for a theory of universal grammar, and it is thus appropriate to discuss specific proposals concerning the substance of such a theory. In particular, we will investigate the theory put forth in Chomsky (1965). Our concerns will center mainly around the organization of the components of a grammar of natural language, rather than with the details of the internal construction of each component, discussion of which is left to other chapters.

In the Standard Theory, the term for the theory of Chomsky's *Aspects*, the grammar of any natural language consists of four different algorithms or computing routines that are articulated so as to provide sound-meaning pairings. A grammar with these components is intended to represent the competence of a native speaker, which is utilized in the actual performance of linguistic behavior: hearing and understanding utterances, and producing utterances with the intended meaning. Each component contains a set of rules which are utilized in derivations from certain initial symbols to certain results. The four components in the Standard Theory are the phrase structure, transformational, semantic, and phonological components. The organization of these components may be visualized by the following flow diagram:

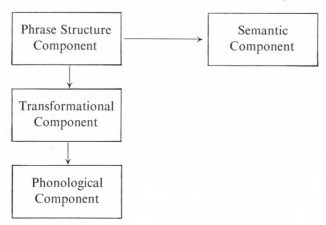

In the chart, the output of the phrase structure component forms the input to the transformational and the semantic components. The transformational component maps deep structures into surface structures by processes discussed in the previous chapter. The semantic component maps deep structures into semantic representations by a set of *projection rules*. The operation of these rules will be discussed in a later chapter, at which point an alternative to the theory of semantics contained in the Standard Theory will also be presented. The phonological component contains rules relevant to determining the phonetic shape of utterances.

Let us examine in greater detail the organization and functioning of the base component. This component contains a context free phrase structure grammar, plus mechanism for effecting lexical insertion. We may consider the following rules as an approximation to the rules for English deep structure.

I. (a) $S \rightarrow NP\ Aux\ VP$ $S =$ sentence
    (b) $NP \rightarrow \begin{cases} \begin{cases} NP\ S \\ N \end{cases} \\ (Det)\ N \end{cases}$ $NP =$ noun phrase
                                                                          $VP =$ verb phrase
                                                                          $Aux =$ auxiliary
    (c) $VP \rightarrow V\ (NP)(NP)$ $N =$ noun
    (d) $Aux \rightarrow T\ (M)(have + en)(be + ing)$ $V =$ verb

The first rule says that each English sentence contains a subject *NP*, an auxiliary, and a *VP*. If *NP* is expanded as *NP S*, a relative clause is generated, as in (1).

(1) *The boy who Jones saw*

The deep structure tree for (1) would be (2).

(2)

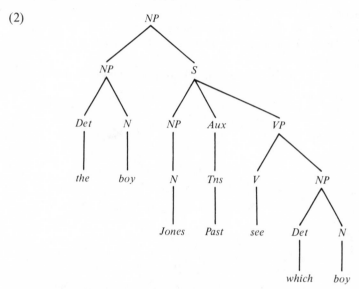

Tree (2) also illustrates *NP* expanded as *DetN* (the boy), and as *N* (Jones), and *VP* expanded as *V NP*. When *NP* is expanded as *N S*, the result is a complement construction, as shown in (3).

(3)

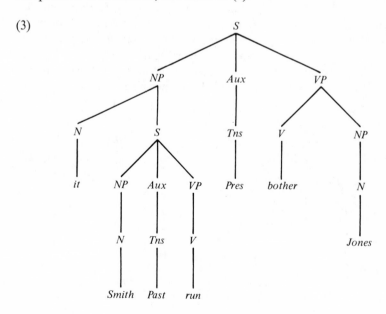

Tree (3) could appear in surface structure as 'That Smith ran bothers Jones', where the 'it' has been deleted, or as 'It bothers Jones that Smith ran', where the sentential complement has been moved to the end by a transformation called *Extraposition*, leaving the 'it' behind. In (3) we also see *VP* expanded as *V* in the embedded sentence. The expansion of *VP* as *V NP NP* occurs in a sentence which contains an indirect object as well as a direct object, as in 'John gave a present to Merry'.

A sentence in which the *Aux* is fully expanded is illustrated in (4).

(4)

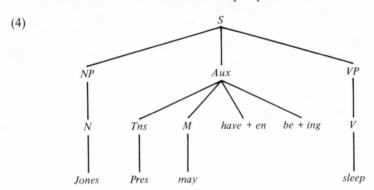

After *Affix Hopping* applies, the resulting sentence is 'Jones may have been sleeping'.

We have made no mention so far of the means by which lexical items are inserted into deep structure trees provided by phrase structure rules such as those listed above. In the treatment of phrase structure grammars in Chapter One, we allowed nonterminal symbols to be rewritten directly as terminals—rules of the form $A \rightarrow a$. Correspondingly, it was assumed in the earliest works on generative grammar that words entered trees in the same way, so that there would be rules of the form $N \rightarrow$ John, $V \rightarrow$ break, and so on. Notice, however, that such rules would permit generation of trees like (5) and (6).

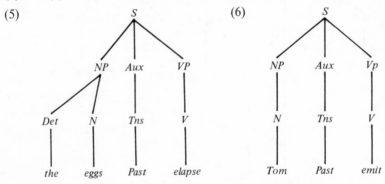

Both *'The eggs elapsed' and *'Tom emitted' are ungrammatical, and to allow their generation would represent a flaw in the grammar. In the theory of *Aspects*, a sentence like (5) is excluded by what are known as *selection restrictions*. Verbs are marked in such a way as to restrict the nouns that appear as their subjects and objects to those that possess the right specification for certain features. Some of the features involved are [± Common], [± Count], [± Animate], [± Abstract], and [± Human]. A noun like 'dirt' is inanimate, nonabstract (concrete), nonhuman, common, and noncount (mass). Sentence (5) would be excluded because the verb 'elapse' requires that its subject be a duration of time. Sentences like (7) are excluded for violations of selection restrictions.

(7) a. *Jones plus two is sixteen.*
    b. *The water scattered on the ground.*
    c. *Mike handed redness to Sam.*
    d. *Tom pummeled sincerity.*

Sentence (7a) is ungrammatical because 'Jones' is not a number; (7b) because 'scatter' requires a count noun subject; (7c) because the object of 'hand' must be concrete; and (7d) because the object of 'pummel' cannot be abstract.

On the other hand, a sentence like (6) is excluded from occurrence through another type of restriction, known as a *strict subcategorization restriction (SSR)*. Speakers of English know (6) to be ungrammatical because an object is missing from the verb. Likewise, a sentence like *'John believed the book to Bill' (patterned after 'John gave the book to Bill') is excluded by *SSR*'s because the verb 'believe' can take only a direct object ('John believed the book'), and not an indirect one.

It is hypothesized in *Aspects* that the constituents a verb can control by means of *SSR*'s are just the constituents of the *VP*. Thus, in the analysis of that work, means adverbials are present in the *VP*, and verbs can be subcategorized for taking them or not. *SSR*'s then prevent generation of a sentence like *'Three hours passed by means of a fork', while permitting 'John ate by means of a fork'.

The grammar of *Aspects*, then, provides for insertion of lexical items into trees generated by the phrase structure rules, providing such insertion does not violate selection restrictions or strict subcategorization restrictions. Hypotheses about language caused by the incorporation of such mechanisms in the grammar have been questioned since the publication of *Aspects*. In particular, it has been argued that selection restrictions are not syntactic in nature, but derive from the meanings of the verbal elements involved. This question will be discussed in more detail later.

4.4

The Evaluation Metric

4.4.1
THE STRUCTURE OF SIMPLICITY

It is possible that even the most tightly constrained universal theory of transformational grammars will not uniquely specify a grammar for each language. That is, the child's language acquisition capacity may be such that more than one grammar is consistent with the data of his linguistic experience, with each grammar generating a corpus not significantly different from the linguistic corpus of the adult speech. The choice between grammars in such a case must proceed on the basis of the structural features internal to the construction of the grammar; i.e., on a basis not connected directly with the sentences generated. The *evaluation metric*, *EM*, in linguistic theory is a hypothesis concerning how the selection proceeds among grammars generating sentences compatible with the same linguistic data. Unfortunately, the terminology suggests that the notion of simplicity involved is some extralinguistic or metascientific notion. That this is not the case will be evident from detailed consideration of various hypothesized *EM*'s below.

There is no claim implicit in the above formulation that any language learner actually constructs several full-fledged grammars, and then compares them, selecting the simplest by the *EM*. Rather, the notion of simplicity applied to a real time model of acquisition would be that the language learner, at each stage in the construction of his grammar, chooses the simplest of any number of equivalent formulations. In fact, it may be that at a certain point in grammar construction the whole system undergoes a radical reformulation in the direction of simplicity, behavioral manifestations of which might appear as temporary retardation in linguistic development and ability. (There is experimental evidence for such "backwards" movement in child language acquisition with respect to, say, understanding the passive construction in English. The correct interpretation of this data is, however, by no means clear.)

The *EM* is universal, its specification being the same for each language. It is inconceivable that the *EM* should receive a different formulation in each language. If we think of a grammar as a representation of the way in which the language learner internalizes his linguistic experience, then to say that the *EM* is language specific is to say, essentially, that it is part of the grammar of each language. Yet the *EM* plays a role of selecting among various observationally equivalent grammars of a given language, and so to say that it is language specific would be to give it the impossible task of selecting for something of which it was a part. Further, means of acquiring a language specific *EM* would have to be universally given. Whatever mechanism is established for this would, in effect, play the role of an *EM*.

In the following we will consider in some detail the internal construction of an *EM* proposed for syntax. The *EM* to be considered is the one worked out in most detail, although the validity of the analysis of the syntactic construction for which it is proposed, the English auxiliary system, has come into serious question in recent work. It is discussed here not as an established area of linguistic research, but rather for the purpose of exemplifying the notion of an *EM*. In fact, the notion of an *EM* has found no productive role in recent syntactic analysis; if deep structure is universal and transformations are also universal as archetypes, then the *EM* will not be accorded a place in the universal theory of syntax.

4.4.2
GENERAL CHARACTERISTICS OF EVALUATION METRICS

EM's which have been proposed for syntax have two parts: a set of conventions for collapsing certain groups of rules, and some counting function which ranks grammars on a scale of complexity. We will take up these matters in turn.

Collapsing conventions specify that certain sets of rules ordered in proximity may be considered to have a special property. Associated with the conventions is a notation for expressing the rules in collapsed form. For example, the convention for conjunctive rules says that phrase structure rules with a common symbol to the left of the arrow may be collapsed in a manner to indicate this common property. The notation associated with this convention is known as the *bracket-notation*. Specifically, rules of the form (8a) are collapsed to a rule of the form (8b).

$$
(8) \quad \text{a.} \quad
\begin{aligned}
A &\to X_1 \\
A &\to X_2 \\
A &\to X_3 \\
&\;\;\vdots \\
A &\to X_n
\end{aligned}
\qquad\qquad
\text{b.} \quad
A \to
\begin{cases}
X_1 \\
X_2 \\
X_3 \\
\vdots \\
X_n
\end{cases}
$$

We interpret rules collapsed by the bracket-notation as in (8b) as applying in the order of their terms from top to bottom.

It may be thought that the notation for collapsing rules, such as illustrated above, is merely a convenience used by linguists for writing rules in a compact form, to save ink on the page, as it were. In fact, such conventions have empirical content, and are intended to express linguistic generalizations inherent in rule systems, and otherwise unexpressed.

That systems of rules that collapse by universal conventions are simpler than systems of rules which fail to collapse, or which collapse less completely, is a function of the operation of the *EM*. The *EM* assigns a value to a grammar on some scale of ranking. A convention for collapsing expresses a generalization under a given *EM* if the complexity assigned to a grammar decreases in proportion to the degree to which the rules of the grammar collapse under the given convention.

It is apparent that there is a rather complex interaction between the formulation of collapsing conventions and evaluation systems for assigning degree of complexity. The *EM* must be designed to reflect the simplicity of systems which collapse maximally by conventions that express true linguistic generalizations. Thus, not every arbitrary notational convention for collapsing rules will be favored by a proposed *EM*. Evidence as to whether some convention expresses true generalizations may be forthcoming from the form of the *EM*, while correct formulation of the *EM* must take into account the necessity to view as simpler those systems of rules that collapse by certain conventions that, by independent evidence, express true generalizations. The dependencies encountered in research on various aspects of obtaining a measure of simplicity are typical of empirical investigations.

Consideration of a few examples may clarify the relation between simplicity measures and collapsing conventions. An extreme case would be one in which something as complex as the phrase structure grammar of English were collapsed by a convention to a single symbol, $\#$. The simplicity of the collapsed system would be great by most reasonable measures, although the saving would be illusory. The convention for expanding $\#$ into a system of rules would not only be intricate, but would also be language specific in the sense of finding application in no other language. Hypothesizing such a convention would involve the prediction that systems of phrase structure rules would tend to evolve in the direction of greater simplicity, i.e., in the direction of collapsibility by $\#$. Stated otherwise, the empirical prediction would be that languages would develop base systems like modern English, a prediction not supported by the facts of language; the convention proposed does not express a true universal generalization about language.

Let us consider another convention whose artificiality is less apparent. Under the proposed convention, rules which had a common symbol on the right of the arrow would be collapsed. The notation for the convention might be as indicated in (9), where the rules in (2a) are collapsed to the rule (2b).

$$(9) \quad \text{a.} \ A_1 \rightarrow X_1 \, B \, Y_1 \qquad \text{b.} \ \begin{pmatrix} A_1 \\ \cdot \\ \cdot \\ \cdot \\ A \end{pmatrix} \rightarrow \begin{pmatrix} X_1 \\ \cdot \\ \cdot \\ \cdot \\ X \end{pmatrix} B \begin{Bmatrix} Y_1 \\ \cdot \\ \cdot \\ \cdot \\ Y_n \end{Bmatrix}$$

$$A \ \rightarrow X \ B \, Y_n$$

Positing this convention involves the factually incorrect prediction that rules having common symbols on the right of the arrow will order themselves in proximity such that they can collapse, for by movement in such direction the total system will attain greater simplicity, by the hypothesis inherent in the convention. Further, according to this convention the maximally simple grammar would be one in which the right side of all rules is the same. Put another way, this convention predicts that adjacent rules will change in a direction of increasing the number of symbols they have in common. Again, such shifts are not observed, and both predictions made by positing such a convention—that rules with a symbol in common on the right will be found ordered in proximity, and that rules in proximity will develop diachronically greater numbers of symbols in common on the right—fail to be borne out. It is thus on empirical grounds that a convention like the one mentioned above is to be excluded from playing a role in the definition of linguistic simplicity.

Most proposals for defining the counting metric involve as part of their formulation that the metric will mark as more complex rule systems which mention more nonnotational symbols, everything else held constant. In other words, it is proposed that the *EM* count the number of nonnotational symbols, i.e., symbols other than the arrow, brackets, etc., as a factor in assigning a rank to a grammar.

Notice that EM's that count symbols find rule systems collapsible by the bracket-notation simpler than systems that do not collapse. Consider two rule systems, such as (10a, b), which differ only in that the first collapses to (3c) while the second does not.

(10) a. $A \rightarrow B \ C \ D$ b. $A \rightarrow B \ C \ D$ c. $A \rightarrow \begin{Bmatrix} B \ C \ D \\ D \ E \ F \\ E \ A \ C \end{Bmatrix}$

$A \rightarrow D \ E \ F$ $B \rightarrow D \ E \ F$

$A \rightarrow E \ A \ C$ $C \rightarrow E \ A \ C$

If we now count the symbols mentioned by rule systems (10a, b) in their collapsed form, i.e., count the symbols in (10b) and (10c), then system (10a) will be valued 10, and (10b) will be valued 12. An EM that uses symbol counting in its operation will rank (10b) as more complex than (10a), given that we collapse (10a) by the bracket notation.

The interaction between certain conventions for collapsing rules and *EM*'s of certain kinds, namely, that rules which collapse are marked as simpler under the EM, is by no means necessary. One can readily invent *EM*'s and conventions for collapsing rules which do not evidence this feature. For example, let us consider *EM*'s that count symbols, but a convention that collapses adjacent rules if (i) these rules can apply in either order, (ii) the output of one rule is never processed by the other rule, and (iii) every string generated by the grammar undergoes application by either one or the other of the rules in the pair. Now, *EM*'s that count symbols would not mark pairs of rules that collapse under the convention outlined above as significantly simpler than pairs that do not, because the number of symbols in the combination of the two rules does not diminish under the kind of collapsing discussed. If it turned out that this collapsing played a crucial role in expressing linguistic generalizations (for which there is, incidentally, little evidence), then an *EM* would have to be devised to reflect this fact.

It is time to turn to a discussion of an actual case in syntactic analysis in which the operation of an evaluation metric may be crucial, and which, correspondingly, may shed light on the nature of *EM*'s in general. The case to be discussed is one of the few, if not the only, case for which convincing arguments could be formulated to demonstrate that an *EM* is in fact interacting with syntactic data particular to a given language to produce an analysis optimal under the *EM*, but not justified alone from the data of the language available to the language learner. It should be remarked that the specific analysis to be discussed, that of the English auxiliary system given originally in Chomsky's *Syntactic Structures* (1957), has been seriously questioned in many recent papers, and is by no means accepted universally. If the *Syntactic Structures* treatment of the English auxiliary turns out to be incorrect, then the considerations adduced below relating to the nature of or even existence of an *EM* for grammars will simply become irrelevant as regards their intended task.

4.4.3
THE ROLE OF SIMPLICITY IN THE ANALYSIS OF THE ENGLISH AUXILIARY

The possibilities for the construction of the English auxiliary in simple declarative sentences is given by a system of phrase structure rules that collapse to rule (11),

(11) $Aux \rightarrow T\,(M)\,(have+en)\,(be+ing)$

where *T* stands for *tense*, and *M* for *modal*. Two supplementary rules expand *T* and *M* as follows:

(12) a. $T \rightarrow \begin{Bmatrix} present \\ past \end{Bmatrix}$

   b. $M \rightarrow \begin{Bmatrix} may \\ can \\ shall \\ will \\ must \end{Bmatrix}$

The past tense forms of the modals listed in rule (5b) are, respectively, *might*, *could*, *should*, *would*, and *must*. The morphemes *en* and *ing* are the past and present participle morphemes.

Rule (11) results from collapsing rules by what is known as the *parenthesis convention*. Stated in general form, the parenthesis convention collapses rules of the form (13a) and (13b) into (13c).

(13) a. $A \to X\,Y\,Z$
      b. $A \to X\,Z$
      c. $A \to X\,(Y)\,Z$

Thus, (11) is the collapsed form of rules (14a–h). Sentences in which the rule given has applied are listed following the rule; in each case below we expand *T* as *present*, and *M* as *may*.

(14) a. $Aux \to T$ It rains.
      b. $Aux \to T\,M$ It may rain.
      c. $Aux \to T\,M\,have + en$ It may have rained.
      d. $Aux \to T\,M\,be + ing$ It may be raining.
      e. $Aux \to T\,have + en$ It has rained.
      f. $Aux \to T\,have + en\,be + ing$ It has been raining.
      g. $Aux \to T\,be + ing$ It is raining.
      h. $Aux \to T\,M\,have + en\,be + ing$ It may have been raining.

The rules given in (14), plus (12a, b), provide for the 48 different possible configurations of the English auxiliary. The rule giving the longest form of the auxiliary (in nonpassive sentences) is rule (14h). When *Passive* applies, a *be + en* appears in final position in the auxiliary. Thus, a sentence like (15a) appears in passive form as (15b).

(15) a. *The architect may have been building the house.*
      b. *The house may have been being built by the architect.*

Consider now the system of rules that results if (14h) is removed from (14). The resulting seven rules collapses by the bracket and parenthesis notations to (16).

$$(16) \quad Aux \to T \left(\left\{ \begin{array}{c} (M)\,have + en \\ be + ing \\ have + en\,(be + ing) \end{array} \right\} \right)$$

Note that under *EM*'s that count symbols, rule (16) is more complex than rule (11). That is, the system of seven rules (14a–g) is a more complex system of rules under a total evaluation metric that uses the bracket and parenthesis conventions for collapsing rules and a counting function to assign relative complexity than is the system of eight rules (14a–h). It is possible to construct a new notation for collapsing rules that will make system (14a–g) just as complex as (14a–h), but use of such a notation would have to be empirically motivated on independent grounds.

Consider next how it is that the child learning English acquires a system of rules that collapse to (11), i.e., rules (14a–h), instead of the more complex (under the *EM* outlined above) system (14a–g). It may be thought that the language learner acquires the full system of the auxiliary by hearing examples of sentences of each type, i.e., sentences like each of those listed in (14). However, sentences in which the auxiliary is fully represented by a modal, perfect, and progressive are vanishingly rare. One computerized sample of more than a million sentences from educated, written text yielded no sentence like the one illustrating (14h). Further, one observer remarked that after eight years of attention to the problem, he had found sentences like (14h) fewer than a dozen times in conversation.

Thus, the evidence indicates that a great many English-speaking children will acquire the full auxiliary system, (14a–h), without having heard sentences directly illustrating each of the rules. Such language learners will be able to recognize as grammatical and understand without difficulty sentences like (14h) without ever having heard such sentences previously. That is, on the basis of hearing sentences which provide direct evidence for, say, rules (14a–g), English speakers conclude that the correct system of rules for the auxiliary is (14a–h).

The hypotheses that the conventions applicable to collapse the rules of the English auxiliary are the bracket and parenthesis conventions, and that the evaluation function counts symbols, explain the above phenomenon. English speakers acquire some subset of rules (14) by direct linguistic evidence, and then deduce the existence of the remaining rules on the grounds of simplicity. They conclude that the total system of rules would be less complex under the *EM* outlined above if the extra rules were present, even though these rules might be directly unattested by observed forms. Under this account, English contains rules (14a–h) rather than, say, (14a–g) on grounds of simplicity internal to the system. Universal considerations dictating the form of the *EM* plus various facts particular to a given language conspire to predict just the right results.

As remarked previously, this elegant account of the relation between the *EM* and the rules for the English auxiliary depends on the correctness of the analysis of this construction given in (11). There is evidence that each of the modal, perfect, and progressive, and also the tenses, occupy positions in deep structure as independent verbs. If the generalization given in (11) is linguistically significant, and not a spurious generalization resulting as an artifact of certain procedures of analysis, and if the evidence alluded to above is to be believed, then some new mechanism of universal grammar must be made available for incorporating this generalization into the grammar of English. Several proposals have been made, but these involve significant departures from the transformational model which has occupied the concern of this book, and so are best left for discussion in a different context.

Formal Deductive Systems

Introduction

In order to understand the construction of the theory of grammar, and the articulation of the component theories of deep structure, transformations, and semantic interpretation, it is necessary to be acquainted with general properties of formal deductive systems. We have already encountered one class of deductive systems in the study of phrase structure grammars; the relevance of the mathematical study of these grammars to empirical considerations in linguistics has been established in the previous chapter. It is hypothesized that deep structure is context free definable, that is, for every language there is a context free grammar that generates the deep structure of that language. Thus, the detailed study of certain classes of context free grammars is of direct empirical significance.

Sets of transformations along with the conventions for their application form another class of deductive systems.

An instructive method for examining the nature of deductive systems is to examine those systems employed in certain formalizations of mathematical logic. Such examination affords one the opportunity to become acquainted with formal languages for logic, which are like natural languages in certain respects. Furthermore, it is possible to recode the usual procedures of natural deduction in logical systems in terms of operations that have many of the formal properties of the transformations of natural language. Working with these operations can provide a backlog of experience in combinatorial manipulation which is essential in the practice of writing transformations of natural language.

The following discussion is devoted to a brief presentation of the propositional calculus and a portion of the first order predicate calculus. The final portion of the discussion concerns general properties of computation systems.

5.2

The Propositional Calculus

5.2.1
THE LANGUAGE FOR PROPOSITIONAL CALCULUS

The usual treatment of this subject begins with propositional letters, p, $q, \ldots$; logical constants, & (and), v (*or*), $-$ (not), $\supset$ (if ... then), and perhaps others; and, perhaps, some parentheses. These signs are considered purely as formal uninterpreted entities; i.e., two strings of such signs are considered to be identical only when they are of the same length and the ith symbol of one string is identical to the ith symbol of the other.

Given the alphabet for the propositional calculus above, one then defines the well-formed formulas (*wff*'s) by rules much like those below:

   (i) **All propositional letters are *wff*'s.**

   (ii) **If φ is a *wff*, then $(- \varphi)$ is a *wff*.**

   (iii) **If φ and ψ are *wff*'s, then $(\varphi \, v \, \psi)$, $(\varphi \, \& \, \psi)$, and $(\varphi \supset \psi)$ are *wff*'s.**

   (iv) **Nothing is a *wff* except as provided above.**

Use of rules like these allows one to specify strings like '$(- (- (p \, v \, (- q))))$', '$(p \supset (q \, v \, r))$' as being *wff*'s, and strings like '——( )', '$- pqr$' as not being *wff*'s.

The language for the propositional calculus being presented here will be specified by means of a phrase structure grammar. In the construction of this grammar given below, it is necessary to provide for an unrestricted number of different propositional letters. (This is the analog of the fact that in building a language for the calculus by well-formedness rules, one usually specifies from the start the existence of an infinity of propositional letters.) This provision is accomplished by the rule which adds primes: $p \rightarrow p'$.

The following is a possible grammar for the set of wff's:

(1) $P \rightarrow (-P)$ (5) $P \rightarrow p$

(2) $P \rightarrow (P v P)$ (6) $p \rightarrow p'$

(3) $P \rightarrow (P \& P)$ (7) $p \rightarrow \bar{p}$

(4) $P \rightarrow (P \supset P)$

In this grammar the initial symbol is P, and the terminal symbols are the logical connectives, the parentheses, and $\bar{p}$ and $'$. In practice below we will use p, q, r, and so on, as substitutions for $\bar{p}, \bar{p}', \bar{p}''$, and so on. One can see in this grammar rules that are analogs of each of (i)–(iii). Namely, (5)–(7) correspond to (i), (1) corresponds to (ii), and (2)–(4) correspond to (iii). Provision (iv) is accounted for by the general provision that nothing is a member of the language of any phrase structure grammar except that which is the last line of some terminated Σ-derivation in the grammar. Let us henceforth designate the language for the propositional calculus by PL.

EXERCISES FOR SECTION 5.2.1

1. Using the grammar given above, give the derivations in tree form of the following formulae: $\bar{p}'''$, $((-(\bar{p} \supset \bar{p}')) v (-\bar{p}))$, $(((\bar{p} \& \bar{p}) v (\bar{p} v \bar{p})) \supset (-\bar{p}))$.

2. Find the nested dependencies in PL which prevent it from being generated by any regular grammar.

3. There is a notation for a language for the propositional calculus known as the Polish notation which uses p, q, etc., as propositional letters, C for the horseshoe, and N for negation. The rules of formation are:

   (i) Any propositional letter is a *wff*.

   (ii) If φ is a *wff*, then $N\varphi$ is a *wff*.

   (iii) If φ and ψ are *wff*'s, then $C\varphi\psi$ is a *wff*.

   (iv) Nothing is a *wff* except by (i)–(iii).

Write a phrase structure grammar which has as its language all the Polish *wff*'s.

5.2.2
TRUTH TABLES

We will first introduce truth tables as they have been presented in traditional treatments of logic. The function of truth tables for the logical connectives is to allow one to assign truth values to a formula of PL according to the possible different assignments of truth value to the propositional letters (atomic propositions) in the formula. For this purpose, two truth values are recognized: T (true) and F (false). One assigns truth values to propositional formulae which are conjunctions, disjunctions, conditionals, and negations by tables (i)–(iv), respectively.

(i)

p	q	$(p \& q)$
T	T	T
T	F	F
F	T	F
F	F	F

(ii)

p	q	$(p \lor q)$
T	T	T
T	F	T
F	T	T
F	F	F

(iii)

p	q	$(p \supset q)$
T	T	T
T	F	F
F	T	T
F	F	T

(iv)

p	$(-p)$
T	F
F	T

According to these tables, a conjunction is true only if both conjuncts are true, a disjunction is false only if both disjuncts are false, and a conditional is false only if the antecedent is true and the consequence is false.

Given the above truth tables, it is possible to assign a truth value to any formula of *PL* once truth values have been assigned to the atomic propositions of that formula. For example, the formula $(-p) \& (p \supset q)$ receives the truth value F when p is assigned T and q is assigned T. This can be seen by observing that when p is T, then $(-p)$ is F, and when p and q are T, then $(p \supset q)$ is T, and, finally, the conjunction of two formulae, the first of which is F and the second of which is T, is itself F, by the table for conjunction. We can represent the results of this simple calculation by a scheme like (v).

(v)

$$-p \ \& \ (p \supset q)$$

$$F \ T \ F \ T \ T \ T$$

In (v), the truth value for a formula is written under the connective for that formula, while the truth value for a letter is written under the letter. Thus, the F under the $-$ of $(-p)$ indicates that this formula is F when p is T.

A chart like (v) can be filled out by assigning the values T, F, F, and F, T, F to p and q respectively. The completed truth table for this formula appears as (vi).

(vi) $(-p)$ & $(p \supset q)$

F T	F	T T T
F T	F	T F F
T F	T	F T T
T F	T	F T F

The process of assignment of truth values to whole formulae of *PL* as a consequence of an assignment to the atomic letters of that formulae can be represented as the assignment of a truth value to a node of the tree corresponding to that formula on the basis of the truth value assigned constituents of that node. For example, given an arbitrary conjunction, the truth table for conjunction can be represented as the following:

(vii)   (a) $P(T)$ (b) $P(F)$ (c) $P(F)$ (d) $P(F)$

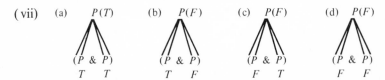

         $(P$ & $P)$ $(P$ & $P)$ $(P$ & $P)$ $(P$ & $P)$
         T T T F F T F F

The parentheses contain the truth value attached to the dominating node when the constituents have the values indicated.

The assignment of truth values in (v) can be represented as assignment to the nodes of a tree according to the truth tables for the elementary connectives (&, v, $\supset$, and $-$), as follows:

(viii)

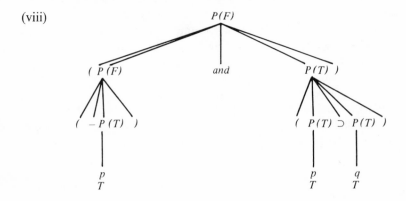

In tree (viii), a truth value is assigned to a node according to the truth tables in terms of the truth value assigned to the node(s) which is (are) dominated by that node. Thus, the P which dominates the first P gets a T, since P has a T. The P dominating $(- P)$ gets an F since, by the truth table for negation, the negation of a T is an F.

The above procedure demonstrates the way in which the interpretation (truth value) of an entire formula is determined by means of the interpretation of its atomic constituents, plus rules of combination. The reader will notice that the logical connectives receive a fixed interpretation in the assignment of a truth value to a whole formula in terms of the truth values assigned to the other terminal symbols. The interpretation of the connectives is provided by the truth tables; the connectives signal, as it were, how the truth values of the constituents of a node are to be combined in the assignment of a truth value to that node. The logical connectives could be thought of as the "function" (versus "content") words of natural language, although the analogy is not complete.

There is a language for propositional logic such that the labels on the nonterminal nodes may be interpreted as the names of the truth tables which combine the truth values of the constituent nodes. In the grammar for this language the logical connectives do not appear as terminal symbols; the function of the connectives is taken over by the labeled bracketing.

To write such a grammar, we let K stand for conjunction ($\&$), D stand for disjunction (v), N for negation ($-$), and I for the conditional ($\supset$). P is the initial symbol, although, as the reader will see, we could just as easily take K, D, N, and I together as initial symbols. The rules for this grammar are as follows:

(ix) $P \to K$ $K \to PP$ $P \to p$

$P \to D$ $D \to PP$ $p \to p'$

$P \to N$ $N \to P$ $p \to \bar{p}$

$P \to I$ $I \to PP$

The only terminal symbols of this grammar are $\bar{p}$ and the prime, $'$. As above, for convenience we will use $p, q, r, \ldots$ instead of $\bar{p}, \bar{p}', \bar{p}'', \ldots$. Using this notation, it is easy to see that the terminal strings of the above grammar are simply all possible strings of p, q, r, and so on. For example, formula (v) above, $(- p) \& (p \supset q)$, would correspond to a terminal string of the form ppq. The logical structure of such a string would be indicated by the tree assigned to it by the grammar. When the string ppq has a structure isomorphic to that of (v), the tree would be (x).

(x)

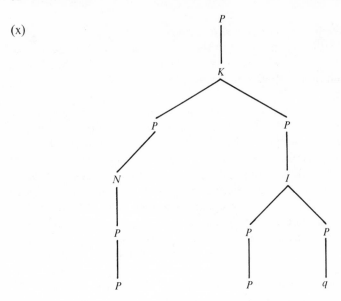

Of course, the string *ppq* is many ways structurally ambiguous in the above
language, as it has a different logical form corresponding to each different
tree assigned to it in the grammar given above. However, the assignment of
truth values to the highest node of a tree like (x) is uniquely determined by the
assignment of truth values to its atomic propositions, as in *PL*.

The interpretation of deep structure in the model of universal grammar
presented in Chomsky (1965) is formally similar to the assignment of truth
values to a formula according to the truth values of the atomic propositions.
That is, a deep structure consists of a labeled bracketing whose terminal
symbols are lexical and grammatical formatives from the language in
question. With such formatives are associated semantic features. Projection
rules assign a reading to a node in terms of the readings of the constituents
of that node, plus, perhaps, the configuration in which these constituents
appear.

One example of such a projection rule is that which produces a set
union of the semantic features of each of a modifier and a head noun. Thus,
the reading assigned to a node dominating 'blue dog', where 'blue' modifies
'dog' in deep structure, is the set union of the readings of 'blue' with those
of 'dog'.

In the Chomsky model the meaning of a sentence is built up from the
meanings of its constituents by projection rules. The process of determining
the meaning of a deep structure by this model is like that of assigning truth
values to formulae in terms of those assigned to the atomic propositions of
that formula. One can find discussion of this sort of interpretation of formal
languages as early as Frege (1879).

An assignment of truth values to the atomic propositions of *PL* is called a *possible world* (cf. Carnap, 1947). The terminology originates from the fact that although some sentence, such as 'Violets are blue', might be true in this world, it is possible that it could be false, so there is some possible world in which it is false. For purposes of interpreting *PL*, a possible world is defined by the sets of atomic propositions in *PL* that are true and false in that world. Some formulae of *PL* are true in every possible world; they are called *tautologies*. For example, $(-p) \supset (p \supset q)$ is a tautology, as evidenced by its truth table worked out below.

(xi) $(-p) \supset (p \supset q)$

F T	T	T T T
F T	T	T F F
T F	T	F T T
T F	T	F T F

A *contradiction* is a formula of *PL* which is false for every assignment of truth values to its atomic propositions. Formula (xii) is a contradiction, as shown by its truth table.

(xii) $(-p) \& - (-q \supset -p)$

F T	F F	F T T F T
F T	F T	T F F F T
T F	F F	F T T T F
T F	F F	T F T T F

A contradiction is false in all possible worlds.

A formula of the form $(\varphi \, v - \varphi)$ is a tautology, where φ is any formula of *PL*. This may be interpreted as meaning that, given a possible world, either φ will be true or $- \varphi$ will be true in that possible world. A formula of the form $(\varphi \& - \varphi)$ is a contradiction, meaning that it is not the case that both φ and $- \varphi$ are true in any possible world.

A formula is *consistent* if there exists an assignment of truth values to its propositional letters which make that formula true. It is evident that tautologies are consistent and contradictions are not consistent. There are sentences which are consistent and not tautologies, however. We might call such sentences *contingent*, as their truth value depends on the selection of the possible world. Each atomic proposition is a consistent, contingent formula.

The partition of the set of all formulae in *PL* into contingent, consistent, tautological, and contradictory formulae is indicated in the chart below.

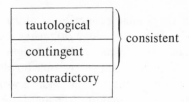

A set of sentences is *consistent* if there is an assignment of truth values to the atomic letters of those sentences which makes all the sentences true at the same time. For example, the set $\{p, q\}$ is consistent, but the set $\{p, -p\}$ is not, although each formula of this set is itself consistent. If a set of formulae is finite, then that set is consistent if the conjunction of all the members of that set is a consistent formula.

Given a set of sentences, Γ, in *PL*, that set has the sentence φ as a *consequence* if φ is true whenever every sentence in Γ is true, i.e., if φ is true in all worlds in which every sentence in Γ is true. For example, the set $\{p\}$ has p as a consequence, and the set $\{p, (-p)v\,q\}$ has q as a consequence. If φ is a consequence of Γ, we write $\Gamma \vDash \varphi$. A set, Γ, which contains a contradiction has every sentence of *PL* as a consequence, for no assignment of truth values to atomic letters of sentences in Γ makes every sentence of Γ true. The empty set has only tautologies as consequences; the reason is that the conditional "if every sentence of Γ is true under an assignment, then φ is true under that assignment" has a true antecedent whenever Γ is empty, because the conditional "if ψ is in Γ, then ψ is true under assignment ζ" is true for all assignments ζ if Γ is empty, since the antecedent will be false.

The logic of the above definition can be spelled out most clearly if we formalize it using the connectives defined for *PL*. Namely, we define $\Gamma \vDash \varphi$, if the following conditional is true: "$((\psi$ is in $\Gamma) \supset (\psi$ is true under $\zeta)) \supset (\varphi$ is true under $\zeta)$." This conditional is of the form $(p \supset q) \supset r)$, which will be true, e.g., if the antecedent $(p \supset q)$ is false.

EXERCISES FOR SECTION 5.2.2

1. Write the phrase marker for formula (xii) above, and work out the third line of the associated truth table ($p = F$, $q = T$) by assigning truth values to successively higher nodes.

2. Show that the formula $-(p \,\&\, (-q)) \supset r$ is consistent; that $(p \, v - p) \supset (q \,\&\, -q)$ is contradictory.

3. Show that: (a) if φ is a tautology, then $\Gamma \vDash \varphi$ for all Γ; (b) if $\Delta \subseteq \Gamma$, and $\Delta \vDash \varphi$, then $\Gamma \vDash \varphi$; (c) it is not generally true that if $\Delta \subseteq \Gamma$, and $\Gamma \vDash \varphi$, then $\Delta \vDash \varphi$; (d) if $\Delta \vDash \varphi$, and $\Gamma \vDash \psi$, for every ψ in Δ, then $\Gamma \vDash \varphi$.

5.2.3
DERIVATIONS IN PROPOSITIONAL LOGIC

Traditional treatments of propositional logic concern themselves with specifying a set of rules, called *rules of deduction*, for deriving formulae of *PL* from sets of formulae of *PL*. In such treatments, the sets of formulae from which deductions are made are called *axioms*, the derivations are *proofs*, and derived formulae are called *theorems*.

The process of deriving theorems from axioms by rules of deduction is formally similar to generating terminal strings by phrase structure rules. In the latter case, the set Σ specifies the axioms, the rules of the grammar correspond to the rules of deduction, and the last lines of terminated Σ-derivations correspond to theorems. The analogy is not accidental. Phrase structure grammars are species of systems developed by E. Post, called Post-systems, for the purpose of modeling deductions in formalized systems of mathematical logic.

In the exposition provided here, we will examine first a system of deduction for the propositional calculus as might be given in a standard logic text, and in doing so we will employ the standard terminology. Second, the system of deduction will be rewritten in a fashion like that used in writing transformations in linguistics. This reformulation of the system of deduction as transformation-like operations is a combinatorial exercise, analogous to translating a program from one computing language to another, and no empirical issues are raised or settled by the fact that deductions in the usual systems of formal logic can be written in a transformational garb. The justification for calling the operations in the revised system of deduction "transformations" is that, like the transformations of natural language, they are mappings from trees to trees. As could be expected, these transformations of logical deductions differ significantly in detail from those in natural language. For example, the output of the deductions of logic are formulae which are themselves generated by the context free grammar that generates *PL*. However, the output of transformational derivations in natural language, called *surface structures*, are significantly unlike the "formulae," called *deep structures*, which provide the input to these derivations. Working with transformations of logic is a useful exercise in becoming accustomed to the customary transformational formalism.

A *derivation* of a formula, φ, in propositional logic from a set of formulae, Γ, by means of a set of rules of deduction, R, is a finite sequence of formulae, called *lines* of the derivation, such that each line is a member of Γ (an axiom), or is derived from previous lines by some rule in R. If there is a derivation of φ from Γ, we write $\Gamma \vdash \varphi$.

We will now specify some rules of deduction of the propositional calculus, dealing first only with formulae containing the logical connectives

$\supset$ and $-$, and leaving until later the extension of these rules to formulae with the other connectives.

R U L E 1 . *Modus Ponens (MP):* If φ and $(\varphi \supset \psi)$ occur as lines of a derivation, then ψ may be entered as a line of the derivation.

R U L E 2 . *Modus Tollens (MT):* If $- \varphi$ and $(\psi \supset \varphi)$ occur as lines of a derivation, then $- \psi$ may be entered as a line of that derivation, and if φ and $(- \psi \supset - \varphi)$ occur, then ψ may be entered as a line.

R U L E 3 . *Negation (N):* If $- - \varphi$ occurs as a line, then φ may be entered as a line, and conversely.

R U L E 4 . *Premise (P):* If φ is an element of the set of premises, Γ, then φ may be entered on any line of the derivation.

The following is a sample derivation using these rules:

(i) $\Gamma = \{ - - q, - (p \supset r) \supset - q, p \}$
    1. $- - q$ P
    2. $- (p \supset r) \supset - q$ P
    3. p P
    4. q $N\ (1)$
    5. $(p \supset r)$ $MT\ (2)(4)$
    6. r $MP\ (3)(5)$

In this derivation the notation in the righthand column indicates which of the above rules was applied in deriving the line to which the notation is appended.

We will now introduce one further rule called *conditionalization* (cf. Mates, 1965), which allows any line to be made the consequent of a conditional.

R U L E 5 . *Conditionalization (C):* If ψ is a line of a derivation, then $(\varphi \supset \psi)$ may be entered as a line, where φ is any formula from *PL*.

Rule C is used in the following derivations:

(ii) $\Gamma = \{ p, - p \}$
    1. p P
    2. $- p$ P
    3. $- q \supset - p$ $C\ (2)$
    4. q $MT\ (1)(3)$

(iii) $\Gamma = \{ (p \supset q), (q \supset r), p \}$
    1. p P
    2. $(p \supset q)$ P
    3. $(q \supset r)$ P
    4. q $MP\ (1)(2)$
    5. r $MP\ (4)(3)$
    6. $(p \supset r)$ $C\ (5)$
    7. $((q \supset r) \supset (p \supset r))$ $C\ (6)$
    8. $(p \supset q) \supset ((q \supset r) \supset (p \supset r))$ $C\ (7)$

Derivation (ii) shows that if a set of premises contains contradictory formulae, p and $-p$, then any formula, q, can be derived. Derivation (iii) shows that $\supset$ considered as a relation between formulae is transitive, in the sense that if we have $(p \supset q)$ and $(q \supset r)$, then we have $(p \supset r)$.

The choice of rules of derivation above is not random; each rule can be thought of limiting possible derivations to those which will derive only true theorems from true premises. For example, MP says that ψ can be derived from φ and $(\varphi \supset \psi)$, and it will be noted that if φ is true and $(\varphi \supset \psi)$ is true, then ψ is true, by the truth table for $\supset$. Likewise, e.g., the rule of negation which derives φ from $--\varphi$, and vice versa, represents the fact that $--\varphi$ is true if and only if φ is true. To conditionalization corresponds the fact that if ψ is true, then the conditional $(\varphi \supset \psi)$ is true for any φ.

The rule of Conditionalization allows the formation of a line of the form $(\varphi \supset \psi)$ whenever ψ is a previous line. Let us establish a convention that if the φ employed in conditionalizing is drawn from the set of premises, Γ, then we will form a new set of premises, $\Gamma' = \Gamma - \{\varphi\}$; i.e., Γ' is formed by removing φ from Γ. We will then say that this line of the derivation is a theorem of Γ' as well as Γ. To state this more concisely: If $\Gamma \vdash \psi$ and $\varphi \varepsilon \Gamma$, then $\Gamma' \vdash (\varphi \supset \psi)$, where $\Gamma' = \Gamma - \{\varphi\}$, and $(\varphi \supset \psi)$ is formed by rule C.

To see this convention in application, consider derivation (iii) above. The part of this derivation which ends at line (5) has all of Γ as its premises; $\Gamma \vdash r$. Line (6) was formed by conditionalizing a member of Γ; at that point of the derivation we then have $\Gamma' = \{(p \supset q), (q \supset r)\}$, and $\Gamma' \vdash (p \supset r)$. Line (7) was formed by conditionalizing a premise out of Γ', so we have now that $\Gamma'' = \{(p \supset q)\}$, and $\Gamma'' \vdash (q \supset r) \supset (p \supset r)$. Finally, the only premise in Γ'' is conditionalized, so $\Gamma''' = \varnothing$, and $\Gamma''' \vdash (p \supset q) \supset ((q \supset r) \supset (p \supset r))$.

It is necessary to place a restriction on the convention for dropping premises after Conditionalization. If a premise is dropped from the set of axioms during the course of a derivation, then the final line of the derivation is a theorem of the reduced set of premises, providing that the derivation subsequent to the Conditionalization does not make use of a line previous to that point that had the dropped formula as a premise. The function of this restriction is to guarantee that only true theorems can be derived from true axioms. The restriction would prevent a derivation such as that below to prove $\{p \supset (r \,\&\, -r)\} \vdash r \,\&\, -r$.

$\Gamma = \{p, p \supset (r \,\&\, -r)\}$

1. p	P
2. $p \supset p$	C (1)
3. $p \supset (r \,\&\, -r)$	P
4. $r \,\&\, -r$	MP (1)(3)

We can conclude from this derivation that $\{p, p \supset (r \,\&\, -r)\} \vdash r \,\&\, -r$, but not that $\{p \supset (r \,\&\, -r)\} \vdash (r \,\&\, -r)$, for, although the premise p could be dropped from Γ after line (2), in which conditionalization applied, line (1), which has p for a premise, was used in deriving line (4). If the restriction on determining what premises are the premises of a theorem is violated in the derivation above, then we will be faced with the undesired result that the last line of the derivation, $(r \& - r)$, can be false, while its putative premise, $(p \supset (r \& - r))$, is true. This situation arises when p is given the value F, and r is given the value either T or F, as is immediately evident from the truth tables for these formulae. By dropping premises from sets of premises by conditionalization, it is possible to produce final lines of derivations which are the theorems of the null (empty) set of axioms. Formulae derived from the empty set by the convention outlined above are called *theorems of logic*. The reader will see immediately that theorems of logic are analogous to tautologies, in that if $\Gamma = \varnothing$, then $\Gamma \vDash \varphi$ if and only if φ is a tautology, and, by the definition, $\Gamma \vdash \varphi$ if and only if φ is a theorem of logic. The meta-theorem of propositional logic which says that the tautologies are exactly the theorems of logic is called the *completeness theorem*. The reader will find it proved in standard works on logic.

Let ψ be any formula of *PL*, containing atomic letters $p_1, p_2, \ldots, p_n$; let $\varphi_1 \ldots \varphi_n$ be any formulae of *PL*. We say that ψ' is a *substitution instance* of ψ, if ψ' is obtained from ψ by substituting φ_1 for p_1, φ_2 for p_2, and so on. For example, let $\psi = (p_1 \supset (p_2 \supset p_1))$, and let $\varphi_1 = (p_3 \supset p_4)$ and $\varphi_2 = (- p_4)$. Then $\psi' = ((p_3 \supset p_4) \supset (- p_4 \supset (p_3 \supset p_4)))$.

It is easy to see that if ψ is a theorem of logic, then ψ' is also a theorem of logic, where ψ' is a substitution instance of ψ. Whatever proof was used to establish ψ as a consequence of the empty set can also be used to establish ψ'. For example, derivations (iv) and (v) illustrate this for the ψ and ψ' given as examples above.

(iv) $\Gamma = \{p\}$ (v) $\Gamma = \{(p_3 \supset p_4)\}$

    1. p P 1. $(p_3 \supset p_4)$ P

    2. $(q \supset p)$ C 2. $- p_4 \supset (p_3 \supset p_4)$ C

    3. $p \supset (q \supset p)$ C 3. $(p_3 \supset p_4) \supset (- p_4 \supset (p_3 \supset p_4))$ C

Notice that any formula is a substitution instance of itself. If ψ contains the atomic letters $p_1 \ldots p_n$, and $\varphi_1 = p_1, \ldots \varphi_n = p_n$, then clearly $\psi' = \psi$.

It is possible now to add an additional rule of derivation.

R U L E 6.   *Theorem of Logic (L): If ψ is a theorem of logic, then ψ' can be added as a line of any derivation, where ψ' is a substitution instance of ψ.*

The application of the rule L is illustrated in derivation (vii), which employs the theorems of logic derived in (iv) and (vi).

(vi) $\Gamma = \{(p \supset q), -q\}$
    1. $(p \supset q)$ *P*
    2. $-q$ *P*
    3. $-p$ *MT*
    4. $(-q \supset -p)$ *C*
    5. $(p \supset q) \supset (-q \supset -p)$ *C*

(vii) $\Gamma = \{-((r \supset s) \supset (-t))\}$
    1. $-((r \supset s) \supset (-t))$ *P*
    2. $(-t) \supset ((r \supset s) \supset (-t))$ (iv)
    3. $((-t) \supset ((r \supset s) \supset (-t))) \supset$
                $(-((r \supset s) \supset (-t)) \supset -(-t))$ (vi)
    4. $-((r \supset s) \supset (-t)) \supset -(-t)$ *MP* (2)(3)
    5. $-(-t)$ *MP* (1)(4)
    6. t *N*

We can now introduce rules for dealing with formulae with the connectives & and v. These rules in essence define formulae with these connectives in terms of formulae containing only $-$ and $\supset$.

R U L E 7.   **If a formula containing a subpart of the form (φ & ψ) occurs as a line of a derivation, then a formula may be entered as a line which is identical to the original, except that the part of the form (φ & ψ) is replaced with a subpart of the form $-$ ($\varphi \supset - \psi$), and vice versa.**

R U L E 8.   **If a formula containing a subpart of the form (φ v ψ) occurs as a line of a derivation, then a new formula may be entered as a line, where the new formula differs from the original by a replacement of the part of the form (φ v ψ) with a part of the form ($- \varphi \supset \psi$), and vice versa.**

Finally, we establish a rule allowing replacement of a subpart, φ, of a formula, χ, with a formula, ψ, if ($\varphi \supset \psi$) and ($\psi \supset \varphi$) are theorems of logic.

R U L E 9.   **If ($\varphi \supset \psi$) and ($\psi \supset \varphi$) are theorems of logic, and if a formula χ occurs as a line of a derivation, where χ contains φ as a subpart, then χ' may be entered as a line of that derivation, if χ was formed from χ by replacing φ by ψ.**

These latter rules can be seen in application in deriving one of de Morgan's laws: that $-(p \& q) \supset (-p \, v - q)$ and $(-p \, v - q) \supset -(p \& q)$ are theorems of logic. The respective derivations proceed as follows:

(ix) $\Gamma = -(p \& q)$
    1. $-(p \& q)$ *P*
    2. $-(-(p \supset -q)$ Rule 7
    3. $p \supset -q$ *N*

$\quad$ 4. $--p \supset -q$ $\qquad\qquad$ Rule 9 $(p \supset ---p$ and $(--p \supset p)$
$\qquad\qquad\qquad\qquad\qquad\qquad\qquad$ are theorems of logic)
$\quad$ 5. $-p\,v-q$ $\qquad\qquad\qquad$ Rule 8
$\quad$ 6. $-(p\,\&\,q) \supset (-p\,v-q)$ $\quad$ C

(x) $\quad \Gamma = \{(-p\,v-q)\}$
$\qquad$ 1. $-p\,v-q$ $\qquad\qquad\qquad$ P
$\qquad$ 2. $--p \supset -q$ $\qquad\qquad$ Rule 8
$\qquad$ 3. $p \supset -q$ $\qquad\qquad\qquad$ Rule 9
$\qquad$ 4. $--(p \supset -q)$ $\qquad\quad$ N
$\qquad$ 5. $-(p\,\&\,q)$ $\qquad\qquad\quad$ Rule 7
$\qquad$ 6. $(-p\,v-q) \supset -(p\,\&\,q)$ $\quad$ C

EXERCISES FOR SECTION 5.2.3

$\quad$ 1. Show that if ψ is any tautology, and ψ' is a substitution instance of ψ, then ψ' is a tautology.

$\quad$ 2. Show that if χ is a tautology, and both $(\varphi \supset \psi)$ and $(\psi \supset \varphi)$ are tautologies, and χ contains φ, then replacing φ by ψ in χ produces a formula which is likewise a tautology.

$\quad$ 3. Show that $(p \supset -q) \supset (q \supset -p)$ and $-(p \supset q) \supset p$ are theorems of logic.

$\quad$ 4. Derive the remaining de Morgan law, namely that $-(p\,v\,q) \supset (-p\,\&-q)$, and $(-p\,\&-q) \supset -(p\,v\,q)$.

$\quad$ 5. If $\Gamma \vdash \varphi$, then there is a finite $\Gamma' \subseteq \Gamma$ such that $\Gamma' \vdash \varphi$.

5.2.4
TRANSFORMATIONAL DEDUCTIONS

This section will be concerned with rewriting the rules of derivation just given in the formalism of transformations. In other words, just as the rules for well-formed formulae in *PL* were expressed as rules in a phrase structure grammar which had *PL* as its language, the rules of deduction will be expressed as transformational rules.

$\quad$ Whereas phrase structure rules are operations on single nonterminal symbols, transformations are operations on whole trees. Transformations operate on input trees in one of a specified number of different ways; they do not operate on all possible trees, but each transformation is restricted to apply to the subclass of trees which meet certain criteria. This will be spelled out by example when we consider the problem of writing specific transformations to mimic rules of deduction.

We have written deductions above as a sequence of formulae from *PL*; in the following representation of deductions, the lines will all be constituents of a tree, so that transformations may refer to previously occurring subparts of that tree in the way that rules of deduction refer to previous occurring lines. Even though the set of premises, Γ, may be infinite in the deductions outlined in 5.2.3, in any deduction only a finite number of premises from Γ are utilized. Thus any deduction performed allowing infinite sets of axioms may be performed by restricting the deduction to a finite set of axioms. (Even though this may not be desirable from the point of view of logic, it is a technical necessity in constructing deductions by means of transformations, as will be seen below.)

All transformational deductions will start out with a finite set of premises, $\varphi_1, \ldots, \varphi_n$. These premises will be dominated in common by the node *Pr* at the outset of the transformational derivation, as shown in (1).

(1)

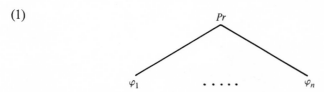

For example, deduction (iii) above, which at an intermediate stage derives *r* from $(p \supset q)$, $(q \supset r)$, and *p*, will start out as (2) when performed as a transformational derivation. (We use *p*, *q*, *r* for the $\bar{p}$'s, as usual.)

(2)

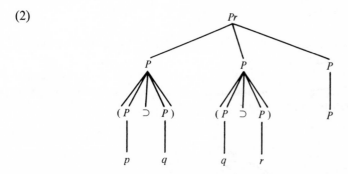

Note that although a configuration like (2) is not generated by the phrase structure rules for *PL*, we could effect its generation by adding a rule schema of the form $Pr \to P^n$, $n > 0$.

The transformational rules which produce lines of deductions will add subtrees to the initial tree of the form (1). If ψ_1 is added as a line, then we will form a tree like (3) from (1).

(3)

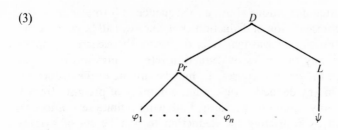

Adding a line consists in transformationally introducing two new nodes, *D* and *L*, in the configuration shown in (3). (No known transformations of natural language operate in precisely this way, although operations similar to this are found.) If we add a line, ψ_2, to (3), we would arrive at (4), and so on.

(4)

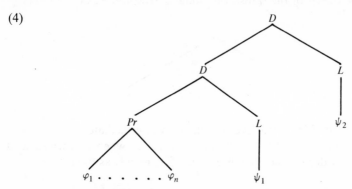

A new *D* is added at each stage to indicate that what is dominated in each case by a *D* is a deduction.

For example, the first line of the transformational derivation corresponding to deduction (iii) is *p*, and so (iii) would be transformed by a rule called Premise (*P*) from (2) into (5).

(5)

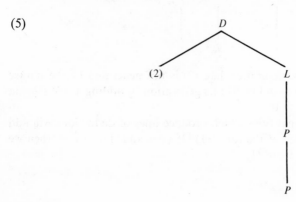

For convenience, tree (2) is represented by "(2)." Let us examine what this transformational rule that corresponds to the *P* rule of deduction looks like.

The transformation rule of Premise $(T - P)$ must allow any constituent of *Pr* to be spelled out as a line. To be more specific, let σ be a string under consideration, and let the operation which builds the nodes *D* and *L* be called *DL*-adjunction. Then the transformation $T - P$ must *DL*-adjoin any constituent directly dominated by *Pr* to the right of σ. Let us use an asterisk * to label the operation of *DL*-adjunction. Then, we can write the operation of $T - P$ in the notation common in transformational grammar in the following way:

Rule 1. Premise $(T - P)$
$$[X_1\ P\ X_2]_{Pr}\ X_3$$
$$\quad 1\quad 2\quad 3\qquad 4 \rightarrow 1\ 2\ 3\ 4\ *\ 2$$

Condition: *Pr* directly dominates 2

The explanation of this notation is straightforward. The X_1 are variables over arbitrary strings of terminals. Note that a variable over such strings is different from a variable over formulae in *PL*. For example, if we are dealing with a transformation that performs some operation on, say, an atomic letter, and so the transformation in part has the form $X_1\ p\ X_2$, then X_1 could assume the value $((- p \supset -$ and X_2 the value $) \supset - r)$ in application to the string $((- p \supset - p) \supset - r)$. The way this string is broken up into a string of the form $X_1\ p\ X_2$ is illustrated in (6).

(6) $((- p \supset - p) \supset - r)$

$\qquad X_1 \qquad p \quad X_2$

Note that neither of the values assumed by X_1 or X_2 is a formula of *PL*. In the same way, the X_1 in Rule 1 are variables over strings of terminals which need not be formulae.

The *P* of $T - P$ stands for the nonterminal of that shape. The rule applies to all trees which may be broken up into four constituents as indicated. The operation of the rule is to *DL*-adjoin the second constituent to the whole string, which is divided up as described. (*DL*-adjunction, as stated, means to place the constituent in question under an *L* node, joining it to the adjacent constituent under a *D* node.)

In $T - P$, the *SD* is $[X_1\ P\ X_2]_{Pr}X_3$, and the *SC* is 1234 $\supset$ 1234*2. The bracketing of $X_1\ P\ X_2$ by a bracket labeled *Pr* specifies that the substring broken up as $X_1\ P\ X_2$ should be exhaustively dominated by a *Pr* node. Variables may assume the null string (string with no symbols) as their value.

For example, when $T - P$ applies to tree (2), X_1 assumes the value $(p \supset q)(q \supset r)$, and X_2 and X_3 assume the null string as values. P assumes the value of the node which dominates p, as indicated in (7).

(7)

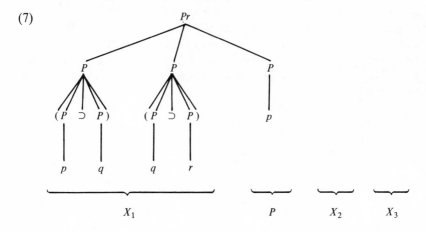

Thus, the tree above satisfies the SD of $T - P$, and the transformation applies, producing (5).

It is obvious that the output of $T - P$ as applies to structure (2) is not uniquely defined, for the tree could be broken up in other ways than that indicated in (7), e.g., as in (8).

(8)

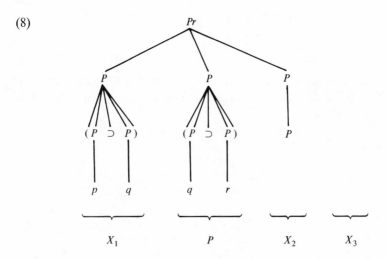

In this case, the output of the transformation would be (9).

(9)

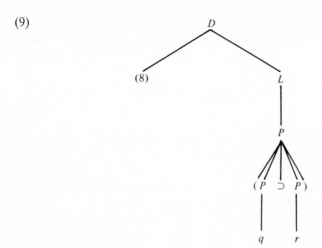

The indeterminacy in the output of $T - P$ when applied to a given string accurately reflects the same indeterminacy in the deductive rule P, which may spell out any premise as a line of the derivation.

The condition on $T - P$ that Pr should directly dominate P is intended to block $T - P$ from breaking up (2) as in (10), which would produce an output like (11).

(10)

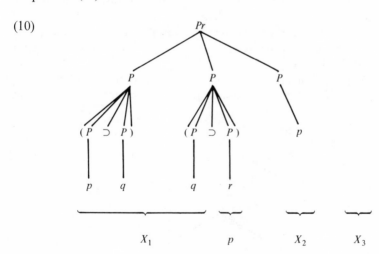

(11)

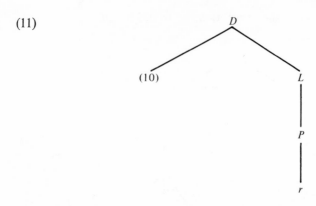

The derivation of (11) from (10) is blocked by the condition that *Pr* must directly dominate the *P* of the *SD* of *T* − *P*. This condition does not obtain in (10), for the *P* which dominates *r* is not in turn directly dominated by *Pr*.

A condition such as that stated for *T* − *P*, that "*Pr* directly dominates 2", is of a sort that is not statable in terms of what are known as Boolean conditions on analyzability. In this way transformation *T* − *P* differs from the kinds of natural language transformations hypothesized to exist in Chomsky (1965). One method to avoid stating this condition as above is to employ what is known as the *A*-over-*A* principle, suggested originally for natural language by Chomsky. By this principle, if a transformation mentions some node, *A*, as part of its structural description, and the transformation is applied to a tree in which such a node dominates itself, then the highest instance of that node must be taken to satisfy the structural description for the operation of the transformation. Thus, a transformation mentioning *A* applying to a configuration schematically indicated below must pick the highest *A* to meet its *SD* (see Ross, 1967, for extensive discussion of the *A*-over-*A* principle).

It is clear that this principle would block derivation of (11) from (10), for in application to (10) *T* − *P* did not operate on the highest *P*-node in the second premise.

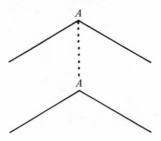

Let us turn next to the task of writing transformations to mimic the operation of other rules of deduction. The rule for negation, being really two rules (to derive φ from $-\,-\,\varphi$, and conversely) will be represented by two different transformations, $T - N1$ and $T - N2$.

Rule 2. Negation

$T - N1 \quad X_1[P]_L\ X_2$
$\qquad\quad\; 1\quad 2 \quad\;\; 3 \;\; \Rightarrow 1\,2\,3 * [([- ([- (\,2\,)]_P)]_P)]_P$

$T - N2 \quad X_1 \quad [(\, - (\, - (\,P\,)))]_L \quad X_2$
$\qquad\qquad\;\; 1 \qquad\quad 2 \qquad 3\ 4 \qquad\quad 5 \;\Rightarrow 12345 \quad * \quad 3$

Rule $T - N1$ has the effect of building a tree containing two negations over any line of a derivation; $T - N2$ has the effect of removing two negations and associated foliage from any line of a derivation.

One case of *modus tollens* (MT) is written as a transformation as follows:

Rule 3. Modus Tollens

$T - MT1 \quad (a)\ X_1\ [\,P\,]_L\ X_2\ [[((\, - P) \supset (- P))]]_L\ X_3$
$\qquad\qquad\qquad\quad\; 1 \quad 2 \qquad 3 \quad\; 4 \;\; 5 \quad 6 \;\; 7 \;\; \Rightarrow$
$\qquad\qquad\qquad\; 1\,2\,3\,4\,5\,6\,7 * 4$
$\qquad\qquad\qquad\qquad\qquad\qquad \text{Condition: } 2 = 6$

$T - MT1 \quad (b)\ X_1\ [[((- P) \supset (- P))]_p]_L\ X_2[P]_L\ X_3$
$\qquad\qquad\qquad\; 1 \qquad\quad 2 \quad\; 3 \qquad 4 \;\; 5 \quad 6 \;\; 7 \Rightarrow$
$\qquad\qquad\qquad\; 1\,2\,3\,4\,5\,6\,7 * 2$
$\qquad\qquad\qquad\qquad\qquad\qquad \text{Condition: } 4 = 6$

We need two different versions of $MT1$, since the lines which serve as the condition for application of the rule may occur in either order. The same is true for MP. In fact, the most convenient way of writing $MT1$ would be to specify either $T - MT1$ (a) or $T - MT1$ (b), as above, indicating that the subtrees labeled L by the bracketing may occur in either order. If the transformations $T - MT1$ and $T - MT2$ were intended to represent the intuitions of logicians concerning derivations, it would be incorrect to have two different rules. Thus, let us devise a notation, $ord(i, j)$, indicating that the terms labeled i and j in an SD may occur in either order. We could then write $T - MT1$ as follows:

Rule 3. Modus Tollens

$$T - MT1: X_1 \ [\ P \ ]_L \ X_2 \ [[((- P) \supset (- P))]_P]_L \ X_3$$

$$1 \quad 2 \qquad\qquad 3 \quad 4 \quad 5 \qquad 6 \quad 7 \qquad \Rightarrow$$

$$1\,2\,3\,4\,5\,6\,7 * 4 \qquad\qquad \text{Condition}: 2 = 6, \ ord(1, 2)$$

The integers above the SD indicate which constituents are subject to the condition $ord(i, j)$. It is easy to see that the predicate ord can be extended from a two-place relation to an n-place relation by defining $ord(i_1, \ldots, i_n) = ord(i_1, \ldots, i_{n-1}) \ \& \ ord(i_{n-1}, i_n)$.

The transformation which mimics conditionalization is a rule schema, representing one rule for each formula of PL.

Rule 4. Conditionalization

$$T - C': X_1 \ [\ P \ ]_L \ X_2$$
$$1 \quad 2 \quad 3 \Rightarrow 1\,2\,3 * [(\varphi \supset 2)]_P$$

For each φ in PL, there is a rule introducing φ as the antecedent of a conditional whose premise is some previously occurring line of a derivation. Another way of effecting $T - C'$ would be to introduce the symbol 'P' where φ stands above, and then allow the phrase structure rules which generate formulae of PL to apply to this symbol, generating some formula *in situ*, so to speak. Either convention will do.

It is possible now to write transformations effecting the deletion of premises when such premises are conditionalized by $T - C'$. Let us call this rule $T - C''$, for the time being.

Rule 5. Conditionalization with Premise Deletion

$$T - C'': [X_1 \ P \ X_2]_{Pr} \ X_3 \ [\ P\ ]_L \ X_5$$
$$1 \quad 2 \ \ 3 \qquad 4 \qquad 5 \qquad 6 \Rightarrow 1 \ \varnothing \ 3 \ 4 \ 5 \ 6 * [(2 \supset 5)]_P$$
$$\text{Condition: } Pr \text{ directly dominates } P$$

When $T - C''$ applies, the premise which is conditionalized is deleted, as indicated by the '$\varnothing$' in the place of '2' in the string representing the *SC* of the transformation.

It is evident by inspection that $T - C'$ and $T - C''$ have part of their environment in common; namely, what is labeled '1 2 3' in $T - C'$ is the same as '4 5 6' in $T - C''$. Furthermore, the operation performed to constituent '2' in $T - C'$ is the same as that performed to the corresponding constituent '5' in $T - C''$. In other words, rules $T - C'$ and $T - C''$ are subcases of a more general rule, $T - C$. We will write $T - C$ as follows:

Rule 6. $T - C$

$$\dashv [X_1 \ P \ X_2]_{Pr} \vdash X_3 [\ P\ ]_L \ X_4 \qquad\qquad \text{Condition: } Pr \text{ directly}$$
$$\text{dominates } P$$

$$1 \quad 2 \ \ 3 \qquad 4 \quad 5 \qquad 6 \Rightarrow 1 \ \varnothing \ 3 \ 4 \ 5 \ 6 * [(\begin{pmatrix} 2 \\ \varphi \end{pmatrix} \supset 5)]_P$$

The brackets $\dashv \vdash$ indicate that the part of the *SD* enclosed need not appear. If the full *SD* is satisfied, then the rule is the same as $T - C''$; if only the latter part of the rule is chosen to apply, then the rule is $T - C'$. The brackets on the right side of the *SC*, $\begin{pmatrix} 2 \\ \varphi \end{pmatrix}$, indicate that 2 is to be entered if $T - C''$ is applied, and some arbitrary φ if $T - C'$ is applied.

We may use the transformations outlined above to execute derivation (11) above as a transformational derivation.

(12)

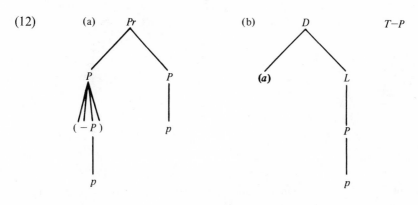

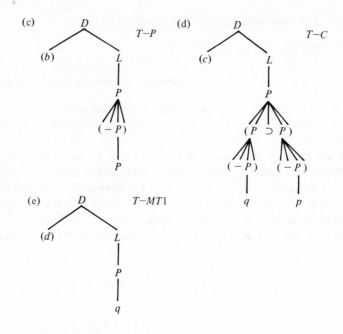

The entire sequence of the deduction is represented in (13).

(13)

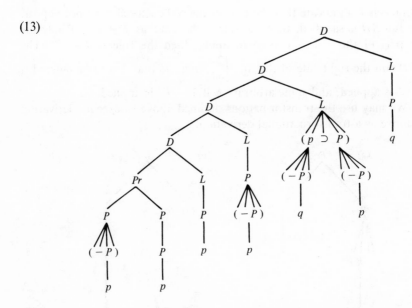

We could go on to conditionalize premises to form, say, (14a) and then (14b), by applying the second case of $T - C$.

(14)   (a)

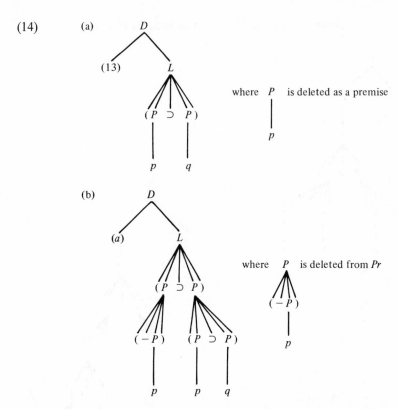

In tree (14b), the *Pr* node is left dominating no constituent. In general, if all the premises of a deduction are conditionalized, the *Pr* node of that deduction will dominate nothing. Thus, we can define a theorem of transformational logic (i.e., logic in which deductions are effected by the transformation-like operations outlined above) to be the formulae dominated by the rightmost *L* node in a derivation whose initial *Pr* node dominates nothing. It is obvious that the class of theorems of transformational logic is exactly the class of theorems of logic defined in the previous section, for any deduction performed by rules of deduction can be mimicked by a transformational derivation, and vice versa.

Let us turn next to the question of writing transformations to effect rules (7) and (8), which allow interchanging subparts of formulae of the form $(\varphi \mathbin{\&} \psi)$ and $-(\varphi \supset -\psi)$ and $(\varphi \mathbin{v} \psi)$ and $(-\varphi \supset \psi)$, respectively.

Rule *T*–7

$X_1 [X_2 (P \mathbin{\&} P) X_3]_L X_4$
1   2 3 4 5 6 7 8   9 $\Rightarrow$
$\Rightarrow 1\,2\,3\,4\,5\,6\,7\,8\,9 * 2\,3 - [4 \supset [(-6)]_p)]_p 7\,8$

Rule *T*-7 would allow a structure like (15a) to become (15b).

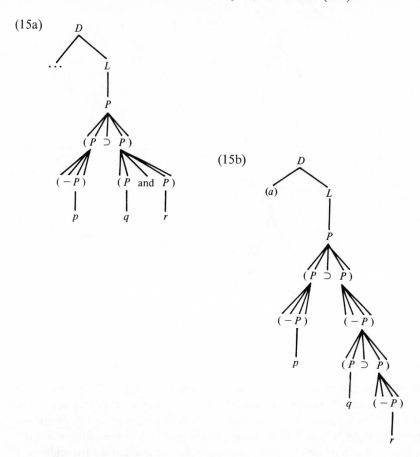

Writing rule (8) as a transformation is left as an exercise.

EXERCISES FOR SECTION 5.2.4

1. Write a transformation to mimic modus ponens (*MP*), and *MT*2.

2. Using the transformations written in (1), complete derivation (iii) in the form of a transformational derivation.

3. Write rule (8) as a transformation.

4. Formulate rules *MP*, *MT*, *C* and *N* for propositional calculus in Polish notation.

5.3

General Properties
of Computation Systems

We have been concerned with the internal construction of various computation systems. All the systems discussed have certain general properties in common, and it is instructive to review these before proceeding with a discussion of another species of logic.

Stated most generally, a computation system consists of a vocabulary, V, along with a specified subset of V called the *initial symbols*, and a set of rules, R. A *computation* is a sequence of strings of symbols from V, such that the first member of the sequence is an initial symbol, and each line is successively derived from the previous line(s) by application of a rule from R. The *upshot* of a computation is the last line of that computation.

We have examined four different kinds of computation systems so far; it is important to see the manner in which each manifests the properties outlined above:

(i) For the phrase structure grammars, the set V is the finite alphabet with which trees of the language are constructed, R is the set of rewrite rules, and the set of initial symbols is denoted Σ.

(ii) In the case of deductions in the propositional calculus, the vocabulary for the computation system is all of PL; that is, the vocabulary is infinite, and is itself generated by a computation system. The initial symbols of deductions in the calculus are likewise formulae of PL, where each deduction or "calculation" within the system proceeds from a set of initial symbols, the set of premises. The rules of the computation system are the rules of deduction. For a fixed set of premises, Γ, we might think of the "language" generated from Γ by the system to be the set of φ such that $\Gamma \vdash \varphi$. This set is known as the *deductive closure* of Γ, and is denoted $D(\Gamma)$.

(iii) The assignment of truth value to formulae of PL in terms of the assignment of truth value to their atomic propositions forms a computation system. The initial symbols of this system are the formulae of PL in tree form with some assignment of truth values to the atomic propositions. (Thus, if some formula has n atomic letters, corresponding to this formula there will be 2^n initial symbols of the computation system, one for each possible assignment of truth values to the atomic letters.) The rules of computation are the truth tables for the logical connectives, which determine how a truth value is to be assigned to some node in terms of the truth values of its constituents. Successive lines in a computation are trees with truth values assigned to respectively higher nodes. A computation in this system is terminated when a truth value has been assigned to the highest node.

(iv) In the system of transformational deductions, the initial symbols are finite sequences of formulae dominated by a *Pr* node, corresponding to finite Γ in (ii) above. The rules of the system are the "transformations," and the upshot of respective computations are whole trees which represent the history of the derivation.

Computation systems are of interest as tools of analysis in linguistics because a computation system can serve as a means of characterizing the results of all computations within that system. In particular, a computation system is capable of providing a finite characterization of an infinite set—the vocabulary and set of rules are finite, the set of upshots of computations may be infinite. Furthermore, each upshot receives a characterization in terms of the computation that leads to that upshot. For example, the string '$-(-p \, v \, (p \, \& \, q))$' in *PL* is characterized by the grammar for *PL* given above as the result of applying the rules $P \rightarrow -P, P \rightarrow P \, v \, P$, and $P \rightarrow P \, \& \, P$ in a certain order. A sentence such as the one you are now reading is characterized by the transformational grammar of English as the result of applying certain phrase structure and transformational rules. A sentence such as 'They are flying planes' is the upshot of two different computations, thus receiving two different characterizations by the grammar of English, one corresponding to each of its possible interpretations.

The linguist attempts to construct a characterization for each language he studies by finding a computation system that generates that language, the internal construction of which is such that it provides a characterization of each sentence that correctly models the speaker's linguistic intuitions. In order to find the right grammar of any language, it is necessary to be able to specify the universal properties of grammars of natural languages. The theory of grammar, then, is the general theory of computation systems for natural languages. The theory is advanced by examining particular properties of individual languages. As the linguist is by necessity concerned with universal grammar, the task of constructing a grammar for a particular language interacts at every point with considerations of universal grammar. Simply producing the optimum computation system to generate certain sentences from a given language is inadequate if the constructed system utilizes devices that are elsewhere unprecedented in language.

The task of learning a language can be viewed as that of internalizing the vocabulary and rules of a certain computation system. Certain parts of the vocabulary of the grammar are hypothesized to be universal; these include the stock of nonterminal symbols. The terminal symbols of the grammars of natural language are clearly language particular, as evidenced by the fact that each language utilizes its own stock of words. Some grammarians working subsequent to the publication of *Aspects* postulate that certain if not all rules of grammar are also universal; this subject will be discussed in a later chapter.

5.4

The First-Order Predicate Calculus

The treatment of the first-order predicate calculus (*FPC*) to follow will parallel that of the propositional calculus. Thus, our first concern will be the specification of a language for *FPC*, both in the traditional manner and as the language of a context free phrase structure grammar. Second, rules of interpretation for formulae of the *FPC* will be given; again, these can be cast in a formalism to render them like the rules of semantic interpretation for natural language envisaged in Chomsky (1965).

The language for *FPC* is more English-like than *PL*. *PL* is a language which reflects certain English constructions involving negation, conjunction, disjunction, and the conditional. There are some differences between *PL* and English as concerns both syntax and semantics. The syntactic differences revolve about the fact that only binary conjunctions and disjunctions are allowed in *PL*. However, there is evidence that English has a construction like (3), e.g., as well as (1) and (2).

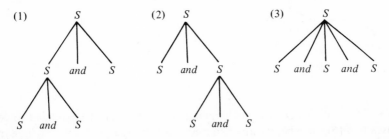

PL requires no ternary branching conjunctions (and disjunctions), since rules of interpretation by means of truth tables, as well as rules of deduction, treat (1) and (2) alike. This is represented by the fact that (4) is a theorem of logic, and tautology.

(4) $(((p \mathbin{\&} (q \mathbin{\&} r)) \supset (p \mathbin{\&} q) \mathbin{\&} r)) \mathbin{\&} (((p \mathbin{\&} q) \mathbin{\&} r) \supset (p \mathbin{\&} (q \mathbin{\&} r)))$

The semantic differences concern the adequacy of the truth tables for representing correctly the semantics of 'and', 'or', 'if . . . then', and 'not' in natural language. Many counter examples can be found in each case. For example, a sentence like 'Either Joe left or Sam left' is usually taken to mean that both didn't leave (as a presupposition). There are cases when it is obvious that a conditional in natural language is not true simply because its antecedent is false or its consequent true. For example, in counterfactuals such as 'If Houston were a suburb of Manhattan, it would be 200 miles from Dallas', the truth of the whole is not some simple function of the truth value of the clauses. In this case, we would count the whole conditional as false, even though the antecedent is false and the consequent is true.

Like *PL*, the language for *FPC* is similar to a part of English syntax, but is by no means an adequate model of English at either the deep or surface levels of representation. The language for *FPC* contains *PL* as a proper subpart, and so all the failings of *PL* are inherited by *FPC*. Further, there is no mechanism in the language for *FPC* to represent the syntax of English sentences such as 'Jones believes there is a unicorn in the garden', in which an embedded sentence appears under a noun phrase object of a higher sentence. That is, there is no formula in *FPC* like (5) to represent the structure of a sentence like (6).

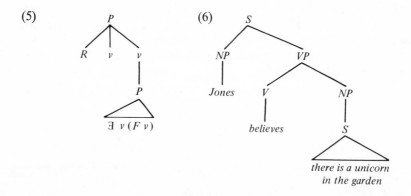

We will not consider how the language for *FPC* might be extended to cover cases like (6), or whether any extension can adequately represent the syntax of English. It is sufficient to remark that although this language is like English in several respects, it should not be interpreted as an attempted model for all of English, or as anything more than a formal language in which deductions in mathematics may be performed.

5.4.1
A LANGUAGE FOR *FPC*

The language for the *FPC* (*LPC*) contains *PL* as a proper subpart. Thus, *LPC* has the alphabet for *PL* as a part of its alphabet; to form strings of *LPC* we add the following sets of symbols to the alphabet for *PL*:

(i) the variable x, which, with the symbol $'$, is used to construct a potentially infinite set of different variables, x', x'', x''', and so on. In practice, we will use such symbols as x, y, and z for variables. We cannot allow an infinite number of variable letters in the alphabet for *LPC* unless the definition of phrase structure grammars is changed to allow infinite alphabets.

(ii) the quantifiers $\forall$ and $\exists$.

(iii) for each n, an infinite number of n-place predicate letters, F_i^n. The superscript indicates how many arguments the predicate letter takes, and the subscript indexes the letter. This doubly infinite array of letters could be generated by a clever us of primes, but there is no need for the excess formalism. We will introduce the following, then, as predicate letters:

$$F_1^1, F_2^1, F_3^1 \ldots$$
$$F_1^2, F_2^2, F_3^2 \ldots$$

$$\cdot$$
$$\cdot$$
$$\cdot$$

$$F_1^n, F_2^n, F_3^n \ldots$$

$$\cdot$$
$$\cdot$$
$$\cdot$$

For added convenience, $F, G, H \ldots$ will be used for one-place predicates, and $R, S, T, \ldots$ for two-place predicates.

(iv) the constants a, a', a'', a''', and so on. For convenience, a, b, c, etc., will be used.

Given these terminal symbols, we add new rules of formation to those for *PL*, as follows:

(a) If F_i^n is an *n*-place predicate letter, and $v_{j_1} \ldots v_{j_n}$ is a sequence made up of variables and constants of length *n*, then $F_i^n(v_{j_1} \ldots v_{j_n})$ is a formula.

(b) If φ is a *wff*, and v a variable, then $(\forall v)(\varphi)$ and $(\exists v)(\varphi)$ are *wff*'s.

It is frequently useful to think of formulae of *LPC* as models of certain kinds of sentences of English. One-place predicate letters correspond to adjectives like 'red' or 'even'; two-place letters correspond to relation words like 'is taller than', 'is brother to', 'is greater than'. The constants correspond to the proper names, such as 'Tom', 'New Jersey', and '2'. The quantifiers $\forall$ and $\exists$ correspond to 'for all' and 'there exists', respectively. Given this correspondence, we can "translate" English sentences into formulae of *LPC*; the formulae are said to represent the *logical form* of the sentences they translate. Some sentences and their translations are given below.

(1) a. *Two is even. F(2)*
     b. *Three is less than six. R(3,6)*
     c. *Something is even.* $(\exists x)(Fx)$
     d. *Everything is even or odd.* $(\forall x)(F(x) \vee G(x))$
     e. *Something is less than six.* $(\exists x)(R(x,6))$
     f. *Everything is less than something.* $(\exists x)(\forall y)(R(y,x))$
                                        $(\forall x)(\exists y)(R(x,y))$

Two translations are given for (1f), as this sentence is ambiguous in English, depending on whether or not the word 'something' is taken as referring to some specific thing.

As remarked above, the first order calculus may be thought of as representing the logical form of sentences of English, in the sense that the logical form of a sentence is taken to be that which is relevant to finding the logical consequences of that sentence. In this respect, (1a) has the same logical form as, say, 'George is tall', which could be translated into *LPC* as $F(g)$. Thus, whatever can be deduced from one can likewise be deduced from the other; $(\exists x)(F(x))$ follows from (1a), and a sentence of the same form follows from $G(b)$.

Formulae of *LPC* specify the logical form of a sentence by abstracting away from what the sentence is about, its content, and leaving only the way the sentence is constructed syntactically. One purpose of early researchers in constructing logical calculi was to show that mathematics could be treated as the study of the consequences of sets of propositions based solely on the logical form of those propositions, without regard to what they were intuitively felt to be about.

There are formulae of *LPC* that correspond to no grammatical English sentences. Examples of such formulae are shown in (2a–c).

(2) a. $F(x)$
     b. $F(a) \ \& \ (\forall y)(R(y, z))$
     c. $R(x, b)$

These formulae share in common the property of containing variables that are not quantified. Frege (1879) termed such formulae *unsaturated*. For example, (2a) might be thought of as similar to an English "sentence" like 'x is red', in which 'x' is a placeholder for the subject of the sentence. Corresponding to such a string there is no assertion; only when the 'x' is replaced by a name, such as 'Paris', or is quantified over by 'there is an x such that' or 'for all x' is there an assertion made.

We may turn now to the task of constructing a phrase structure grammar to generate *LPC*. This grammar contains all the rules for *PL*, plus those specified below. Its terminal vocabulary will be augmented by the symbols listed above; its nonterminal vocabulary will be augmented by the symbols Q (quantifier) and v.

(a) $P \rightarrow F_i^n(\overbrace{v \ldots v}^{n})$
(b) $v \rightarrow x_i, v \rightarrow a_i$
(c) $P \rightarrow (Qx_i)(P)$
(d) $Q \rightarrow \forall, Q \rightarrow \exists$

Rule scheme (a) rewrites P as an n-place predicate letter followed by n v's, where each v can be a variable or a constant, as allowed by (b). Rules (c) and (d) introduce quantifiers.

Using these rules, we assign trees (3a, b) to the different readings for (1f) above.

(3)

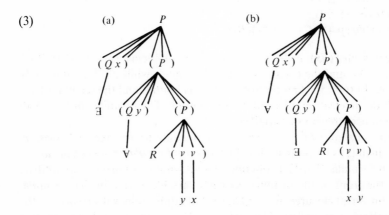

Formulae (4a, b) have tree structures indicated in (5a, b) respectively.

(4)   a. $(\exists x)(F(x) \,\&\, G(x))$
      b. $(\exists x)(F(x)) \,\&\, (\exists x)(G(x))$

(5)

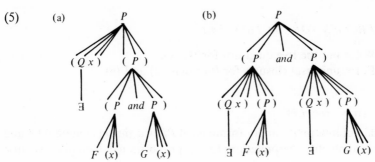

The different trees for (4a, b) represent the inherent difference in meaning between these formulae. The first says that something is both F and G, while the second asserts only that something is F, and something else (not necessarily distinct) is G.

The *scope* of a quantifier node, Q, is defined to be the phrase marker which is dominated by the node which dominates that quantifier node. Thus, the scope of the existential quantifier in (3a) is the whole tree, whereas that of the existential quantifier in (3b) is the subtree $(R(x, y))$. If the variable x_i occurs immediately adjacent to a Q node, we say that the quantifier dominated by Q *quantifies over* x_i in the scope of Q. A variable x_i in a formula is *free* if it is not quantified over by a quantifier in some occurrence in that formula. If x_i is in the scope of a quantifier over x_i in some occurrence, we say it is *bound* in that occurrence. Consider now (6a–c):

(6)   a. $(\exists x)(\forall y)((Fx \, v \, Gx) \supset (Gy \, \& \, Fz))$
      b. $(\forall x)(Fx) \, \& \, Gx$
      c. $(\exists x)(\forall y)(\exists z)(Gx \supset (\exists w)(Ryz \supset F_w))$

(In (6) we write (Fx) instead of $(F(x))$ for convenience.) In (6a) both occurrences of x and the occurrence of y are bound, while z is free in its only occurrence. In (6b), the first occurrence of x is bound, and the second is free. In (6c) all occurrences of all variables are bound. The formulae in (2a–c) all contain free occurrences of variables.

A formula of *LPC* is a *sentence* if it contains no free variables. A formula which is not a sentence is called an *open formula*. A *universal closure* of an open formula of *LPC* is obtained by appending a universal quantifier, $(\forall x_i)$, to the front of the formula for each variable x_i free in that formula. Different universal closures of an open formula differ only with respect to the order of the initial universal quantifiers. For example, (7b, c) are two different universal closures of (7a).

(7)   a. $(\exists x)(R(xy) \, \& \, (F(z)))$
      b. $(\forall y)(\forall z)(\exists x)(R(x, y) \, \& \, F(z))$
      c. $(\forall z)(\forall y)(\exists x)(R(x, y) \, \& \, F(z))$

EXERCISES FOR SECTION 5.4.1

1. Write out the tree diagrams for (6a–c).
2. Form universal closures for formulae (2) and (6).

5.4.2
INTERPRETATIONS FOR *LPC*

The domain of interpretation for formulae of *PL* was the set containing T and F. In providing an interpretation for a propositional formula, we first assigned each atomic letter of that formula to some truth value, and then worked up the tree, assigning truth values to successively higher nodes in accordance with the truth tables. The truth value assigned to the whole formula was that assigned to the highest node of the formula.

The same process is applied in finding interpretations for formulae of *LPC*; in addition, we add mechanism to assign readings for formulae of the form $F_i^n(v \ldots v)$, where each v is a variable or a constant. These correspond to the atomic letters of *PL*. We also need mechanism to assign truth values to quantified formulae. It is instructive to proceed informally in constructing the required mechanism, and to attempt a formalization of this construction only after the intuitive content of the formalism is apparent.

We begin by considering formulae like $F_i^n(v \ldots v)$. Consider instances of these, such as (8a, b).

(8) a. $F(a)$
     b. $R(b, c)$

In (8) there are no variables; the interpretation of formulae with variables will be considered when we deal with quantifiers. The constants, a, b, c, etc., may be thought of as names of objects; one-place predicate letters as names of predicates; two-place predicate letters as names of relations between pairs of objects; and, in general, n-place predicate letters may be thought of as representing relations between sets of n-objects considered in some order, called n-tuples of objects.

Thus, to interpret formulae like (8), we need some domain of objects, D, which the constants may name, and sets of which the letters may represent. The domain D is called the *domain of discourse* for an interpretation of *LPC*. The constants are assigned a fixed denotation in each domain which serves as an interpretation for *LPC*; each predicate letter is also assigned a fixed property of n-tuples in D. When we consider properties in D, however, we treat them in extension. That is, instead of speaking of F, say, as representing the property of "being even" when *LPC* is interpreted in the domain of natural numbers, we speak of F as representing the set of even numbers. In general, the extension of a property is the set of things (1-tuples) which have that property; the extension of a two-place relation is the set of ordered pairs (2-tuples) which enter into that relation. Thus, if *LPC* were to be interpreted in the domain of physical objects, a one-place predicate letter, such as G, would represent the property of "being red" by denoting the set of red objects. The two-place letter S would represent the property of "being smaller than" by denoting the set of ordered pairs, such that the first member of each ordered pair is smaller than the second member.

Let *LPC* be interpreted in the domain of natural numbers, let F denote the set of even numbers, G the set of odd numbers, R the set of ordered pairs of numbers such that the first is less than the second, a the number 1, b the number 2, and c the number 3. Then formula (8a) would be false, since 1 is not even; (8b) would be true, since 2 is less than 3. Phrased differently, (8a) is false because the object denoted by a is not a member of the set denoted by F; (8b) is true because the ordered pair, (2, 3), is an element of the set of ordered pairs denoted by r. Likewise, formulae (9a, b, c) are respectively true, true, and false.

(9)   a. $F(a) \vee G(a)$
      b. $F(a) \supset R(a, c)$
      c. $R(a, b) \supset R(b, a)$

Formula (9a) says that 1 is either even or odd, and is true because the second member of the disjunct is true, by the truth tables. Formula (9b) states that if 1 is even, then 1 is less than 3, which is true, again by the truth tables. And (9c) states that if 1 is less than 2, then 2 is less than 1, a falsehood.

We can now formalize the portion of the interpretation of *LPC* discussed above: Let D be a domain. An interpretation of *LPC* is some assignment, f, which assigns constants (names) to objects in D, one-place letters to sets in D, two-place letters to sets of ordered pairs in D, and, generally, n-place predicate letters to sets of n-tuples in D. A formula such as $F(a)$ will be true under this interpretation in D, if the object denoted by a under f is an element of the set denoted by F; i.e., $F(a)$ is true if and only if $f(a) \in f(F)$. A formula like $R(a, b)$ will be true if the pair of objects denoted by a and b is in the set of ordered pairs denoted by R; $R(a, b)$ is true if and only if $(f(a), f(b)) \in f(R)$. In general, then, $F_i^n(a_{i_1}, \ldots, a_{i_n})$ is true if and only if $(f(a_{i_1}), \ldots, f(a_{i_n})) \in f(F_i^n)$.

Suppose we treated English as an *LPC*, where the domain of interpretation is all the things English is used to talk about. Then, the word 'red' would denote the set of red objects, and a two-place relation word like 'is a brother of' would denote the set of ordered pairs of males, the first of which is a brother of the second. 'Tom' would denote Tom, 'Dick' Dick, 'Harry' Harry, and so on. A sentence like 'Tom is the brother of Dick' would be true if Tom is the brother of Dick (see Tarski, 1935). Notice that when English is treated like an *LPC*, not all nouns correspond to phrases which denote individuals; in fact, only proper nouns do. Common nouns are interpreted in the same way as predicates. That is, (10a) and (11a) are treated like formulae of the form (10b) and (11b).

(10) a. *Tom is a man.*
      b. $M(t)$
(11) a. *Susie met a man.*
      b. $(\exists x)(T(s, x) \ \& \ M(x))$

Here, $M = man$, $T = meet$, $t = Tom$, and $s = Susie$. The surface structure noun phrase 'a man' in both (10) and (11) functions as a predicate when we interpret English in the same way as that sketched for *LPC* above. Likewise, in a phrase like 'the man who Susie met', the noun 'man' functions semantically like a predicate, although different analyses provide different logical interpretations for phrases of this sort. (For a discussion, see Carnap, 1946.)

We may turn next to the question of the assignment of an interpretation to quantified formulae. We want an existential formula such as $(\exists x)(F(x))$ to be true if there is something in the domain of discourse which is an F, i.e., which is in the set assigned to F by f. Let us stipulate that corresponding to each variable x in *LPC*, there will be a new constant $\bar{x}$. Put differently, then, $(\exists x)(F(x))$ will be true if it is possible for f' to assign a value to $\bar{x}$ such that $F(\bar{x})$ is true, i.e., $f'(\bar{x}) \in f'(F)$, where f' differs from f only in what f' assigns to $\bar{x}$. That is, an existential formula will be true under f if there is some assignment f' which can find a denotation for $\bar{x}$ which satisfies the formula.

The question of the interpretation of existential formulae can perhaps best be clarified as follows: An existential formula $(\exists x)(F(x))$ is true if the formula $F(\bar{x})$ can be true for some interpretation of the language. In other words, we can make the existential formula true under f if we can find an assignment f' that differs from f only on what it assigns to $\bar{x}$, such that $F(\bar{x})$ is true under f'. If there is such an f', then there must be an object in the domain which is an element of the set denoted by F under f.

These remarks need to be generalized to treat formulae which have more than one occurrence of a variable under the scope of a given quantifier. A formula in which x occurs free will be denoted φx. Then $\varphi\bar{x}$ denotes that formula in which x is replaced by the constant $\bar{x}$. We can say that $(\exists x)\varphi x$ is true under f only if $\varphi\bar{x}$ is true under some assignment f' which is just like f except for what $\bar{x}$ denotes in the domain. We can likewise define $(\forall x)\varphi x$ to be true if $\varphi\bar{x}$ is true for all assignments f' which differ from f only in what is picked out as the object assigned to $\bar{x}$.

The remarks above concerning the interpretation of *LPC* can be summarized in the following. An *interpretation* for *LPC* is a domain D, and a function f which meets the following conditions:

(i) if a is a constant, then $f(a) \in D$.

(ii) if F_i^n is an n-place predicate letter, then $f(F_i^n)$ is a set of n-tuples from D.

(iii) $f(F_i^n(a_{i_1} \ldots a_{i_n})) = T$ iff $(f(a_{i_1}) \ldots f(a_{i_n})) \in f(F_i^n)$.

(iv) $f((\exists x)(\varphi x)) = T$ iff there is an interpretation f' which differs from f only in the assignment of $\bar{x}$ which makes $\varphi\bar{x}$ true.

(v) $f((\forall x)(\varphi x)) = T$ iff all interpretations f' which differ from f only in the assignment of $\bar{x}$ make $\varphi\bar{x}$ true.

(vi) if p is an atomic letter, $f(p) = T$ or $f(p) = F$.

(vii) $f(-\varphi) = T$ iff $f(\varphi) = F$.

(viii) $f(\varphi \mathbin{\&} \psi) = T$ iff $f(\varphi)$ and $f(\psi) = T$.

(ix) $f(\varphi \mathbin{v} \psi) = T$ iff $f(\varphi) = T$ or $f(\psi) = T$.

(x) $f(\varphi \supset \psi) = T$ iff $f(\varphi) = F$ or $f(\psi) = T$.

Terms (vii)–(x) above simply restate the truth tables. Further, it is clear that open formulae receive no interpretation under f; this corresponds to the intuition that a sentence like 'x is red' cannot be used to make an assertion, because it doesn't "talk about" anything. Only when x is quantified over or replaced by a constant is some assertion made.

Let us now use the rules for f to work through the construction of an assignment for formulas like (12a, b).

(12) a. $(\forall x)(\exists y)(R(x, y))$
       b. $(\exists y)(\forall x)(R(x, y))$

Let us think of these formulae as being interpreted over the natural numbers, where R stands for the less than relation. Then f makes (12a) true if (12c) is true for every f'; (12c) is true under some f' if (12d) is true for some f''.

(12) c. $(\exists y)(R(\bar{x}, y))$
       d. $R(\bar{x}, \bar{y})$

Put in words, (12a) is true if for each natural number denoted by $\bar{x}$ under an f' we can find a natural number denoted by $\bar{y}$ under f'' such that the first is less than the second.

Likewise, (12b) will be true if (12e) is true under some f', which in turn will be true if (12d) is true under all f'' for that fixed f'.

(12) e. $(\forall x)(R(x, \bar{y}))$

Put in words, (12b) will be true if we can find a number (assigned to $\bar{x}$ under f') such that (12d) is true for all assignments to $\bar{y}$ by f''. Thus, in the domain stipulated, (12a) is true, but (12b) is false, since no natural number is greater than every other natural number.

EXERCISES FOR SECTION 5.4.2

1. Let $D = (1, 2, 3, \ldots)$ be the domain of discourse, where F denotes the set of even numbers, G the set of odd numbers, R the set of ordered pairs such that the first is less than the second, a the number 1, b 2, c 3, etc.,

under f. Then write out the following formulae in tree form, writing in the assignments provided by f to each node of the tree.

(a) $(\exists x)(R(a, x)\ \&\ R(x, b))$
(b) $(\forall x)(R(b, x) \supset R(b, a))$
(c) $(\exists x)(F(x))\ \&\ (\exists x)(G(x))$
(d) $(\exists x)(F(x)\ \&\ G(x))$

2. Translate the following English sentences into their "logical form" in LPC, where L denotes 'loves', M 'men', and W 'women'.

(a) *All men are not women.* (Ambiguous, find both readings)
(b) *Some man loves all women.*
(c) *A man who loves a woman doesn't love all women.*
(d) *All women love some man.* (Ambiguous, find both readings)

VI

Three Theories of Semantics

Introduction

This chapter will outline briefly the origins and development within generative grammar of three different theories of the semantics of natural language. The formal material provided in the previous chapters, particularly the chapter on logic, provides the necessary background for the discussion.

It will be noticed in the following pages that each theory of meaning is closely articulated with some independently developed theory of syntax. In particular, each case displays a different theory of the role of underlying structure and transformations. Tagging along with each theory, as it were, is a theory of semantics, or, in some cases, what a theory of semantics would look like if it were developed within the particular theory of syntax at hand.

6.2

The Theory of Syntactic Structures

The earliest theory of generative grammar, that of *Syntactic Structures* (Chomsky, 1957), was cast in a form different from that of the later *Aspects*, discussed above. It is worthwhile to outline several aspects of this theory relevant to the theory of semantics that accompanied it. The theory included phrase structure rules, although context sensitive as well as context free rules were allowed, and lexical insertion was accomplished by means of phrase structure rules that rewrote nonterminals directly as terminals (words). Two kinds of transformations were hypothesized to exist: singulary and generalized. Singulary transformations operated in the domain of simple sentences (sentences with no embedded sentences, i.e., in which the only S node was the highest).

In the *Syntactic Structures* theory, recursion was contained in the transformational component. That is, the phrase structure rules generated only a finite language, presumably all the different simple sentence types extant in the language; there was no way in which some nonterminal in a tree generated by this grammar could dominate itself. Generalized transformations performed the function of, as it were, pasting together simple sentences to form complex sentences.

For example, in generating a sentence like 'They believe that $2 + 2 = 4$', which contains two sentences—'They believe . . .' and '$2 + 2 = 4$'—the phrase structure rules generated each simple sentence independently. The *NP* object of the 'believe' sentence contained a dummy symbol. A generalized transformation then substituted the sentence '$2 + 2 = 4$' for this dummy symbol.

It will be noted that in a theory such as that sketched here there is no transformational cycle in syntax. Each tree generated by the base rules consisted of only a simple sentence. Complex sentences were built up from simple ones, with no particular constraints on the order in which sentences were embedded in others, other than those provided by formal devices known as *T*-markers (transformation markers), the details of which need not be of concern here. In the later *Aspects* theory, the generalized transformations are totally lacking; subordinate clauses are generated in their position of embedding by the phrase structure rules.

We can turn now to a discussion of the semantic theory that was tied to this theory of syntax. The application of certain rules was obligatory for the grammaticality of the sentence generated, while the application of other rules was optional. Each phrase structure and transformational rule was marked as to whether it was optional or obligatory; the obligatory rules had to apply in each sentence of the language. Among the phrase structure rules, for example, the rule $S \rightarrow NP\ VP$ would be obligatory. Likewise, the transformation of *Affix Hopping* discussed earlier is obligatory.

In the *Syntactic Structures* theory of semantics, the meaning of a sentence was some function of the set of optional rules that applied in forming that sentence, plus, perhaps, their order of application. It was argued that the application of an obligatory rule could not contribute to the meaning of a sentence, since the well-formedness of the sentence is dependent on the application of that rule, and nothing about the meaning could be determined merely from the fact that that sentence was well-formed. For example, nothing particular to the meaning of 'Jones slept' is dependent on the fact that it is of the form $NP\ VP$, i.e., that the phrase structure rule $S \rightarrow NP\ VP$ has applied in its derivational history.

On the other hand, it was thought that the meaning of a sentence was dependent on the set of optional rules that had applied in its derivation. Sentences like 'The dog ran' and 'The cat ran' differ in meaning, and contain different lexical items in subject position. This difference would be attributable to the fact that different phrase structure rules had applied in the formation of each sentence: $N \rightarrow$ dog in one and $N \rightarrow$ cat in the other. Similarly, questions were derived the corresponding declaratives by an optional transformation of question formation. This transformation directly related sentences like 'John was seen' and 'Was John seen?' It was argued that the difference in meaning between questions and declaratives resided in the fact that an optional rule had applied in one that had not applied in the other.

Passive was optional in *Syntactic Structures*, and it was argued that a meaning difference is at least possible between certain active sentences and their passives. The examples cited consisted of sentences like (1a, b).

(1)   a. *Everyone in the room speaks two languages.*
      b. *Two languages are spoken by everyone in the room.*

A reading of (1a) can make it seem possible for each person to speak two different languages, while (1b) can seem to imply that the languages are the same two languages for everyone in the room.

The difference in meanings of (1a, b) is clearly attributable to the different order of quantifiers: 'For everyone there exists two languages' versus 'there exists two languages such that for everyone'. The representation of difference in scope of quantifiers is correctly made by means of tree diagrams. Thus, it is clear that unless the optional application of *Passive* could be correlated in some way with different tree diagrams for (1a, b) in which the quantifiers had different scopes, this theory would be unable to characterize adequately the difference between sentences like (1a, b). No such attempt was in fact made, and it is not even clear that the problem was perceived in that framework. In any case, the theory of *Syntactic Structures* was replaced by a theory in which semantic interpretation of deep structure was accomplished in a special component of the grammar. We may turn now to an examination of the details of that theory.

6.3

The *Aspects* Theory

The theory of semantics of *Aspects* was based on earlier work by Katz, Fodor, and Postal. In this theory, each lexical item is associated with a set of syntactic, semantic, and phonological features. The phonological features determine the phonological properties of a word, including its final pronunciation. The syntactic features govern the word's syntactic behavior, and the semantic features contain a representation of the meaning of the word.

After generation of a deep structure tree by the phrase structure rules, and lexical insertion by the principles discussed earlier, the resulting full deep structure is processed by the semantic component. Rules of this component are called *projection rules*, and operate in a means that is formally similar to the operation of the rules in the propositional calculus that assign truth values to a node according to the truth values that occur on the constituents of that node, plus the rule of combination of truth values associated with the logical connective, which rule is expressed in truth table form.

That is, in its most abstract form, a projection rule takes a structure like (1) and assigns a semantic reading to the higher node in terms of the readings assigned to the lower nodes, where the rule of combination, the projection rule, is determined from the phrase structure configuration.

(1)

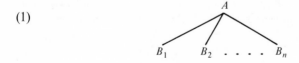

$$A$$
$$B_1 \quad B_2 \quad \ldots \quad B_n$$

Let us consider a concrete example, one of the few examples of projection rules that have been offered by the proponents of the theory of semantics under consideration (known as *interpretive semantics*, as it postulates the existence of semantic rules that "interpret" deep structures, i.e., map them into semantic representation). The rule we will examine is that associated with modifier-head constructions, e.g., adjective-noun.

(2)

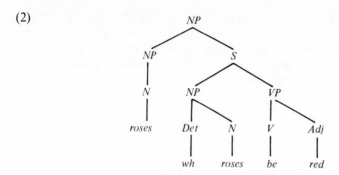

Constructions such as (2) are mapped by well-known transformations into structures like (3).

(3)

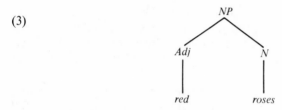

The semantic projection rule in question assigns a reading to the highest *NP* node in (2), which consists of the set union of the features which occur on the head (*roses*) with those that occur on the modifier (*red*).

In interpretive semantics, the projection rules work up through a deep structure tree, assigning readings to nodes in terms of the readings on the constituents of those nodes, until the highest node, *S*, is reached. The reading assigned to *S* is the meaning of the sentence. Within this theory it is possible to take first steps toward a formal definition of semantic notions such as synonymy, analyticity, and contradiction.

A sentence which is of the Subject-Predicate form can be defined to be analytically true if the semantic markers assigned to the predicate are a subset of those assigned to the subject. A sentence like 'Bachelors are unmarried' is marked as analytic, as part of the semantic specification of 'bachelor' is 'unmarried' and 'male', which contains as a subset the markers on the predicate, 'unmarried'. Two sentences are synonymous simply if they are assigned identical semantic readings by the projection rules.

In the theory of *Aspects* it is hypothesized that transformations do not change meaning. This so-called Katz-Postal hypothesis means, intuitively, that the output of the application of a transformation has the same meaning as the input. We may take as an example the *Passive* transformation that relates pairs of sentences like 'John saw a unicorn' and 'A unicorn was seen by

John'. We may state the Katz-Postal hypothesis more formally as follows: If two different surface structures are derived transformationally from the same deep structure, then those two surface structures have the same meaning.

It follows from this hypothesis about transformations that the entire meaning of a sentence is contained in its deep structure, for the application of a transformation could not add to, subtract from, or alter the meaning of a sentence in any way. It was necessary for Katz and Postal to defend their hypothesis by showing that cases which were thought to involve a transformational change in meaning could be reanalyzed otherwise. In the earlier *Syntactic Structures* theory, negatives were formed by means of the operation of a transformation which inserted the negative material into a positive sentence; sentences like 'It is raining' and 'It is not raining' were transformationally related by the transformation that inserted 'not'. Katz and Postal argued that in this case the deep structure contained a negative element. Thus, whereas in the earlier theory there was one "deep structure" (kernel sentence) which received a negative element by the optional application of some transformation, in the later theory there was an optional phrase structure rule which inserted negation into deep structure, and a later transformation that obligatorily placed the negative morpheme into correct position in the surface structure. In summary, the later theory differs from the earlier in its treatment of negation in that what appeared earlier as an optional transformation that changed meaning was handled later by an optional phrase structure rule coupled with an obligatory transformation.

We have examined the application of the Katz-Postal hypothesis to the treatment of negation in detail in order to see what consequences follow in terms of the transformational treatment of English. The treatment given to negation in grammars written following formulation of Katz-Postal hypothesis carries over to other areas of grammar. Thus, in the earlier theory questions were formed from their corresponding declaratives by a transformation whose application was optional. Such an analysis is clearly impossible in a grammar in which transformations preserve meaning, since questions and statements differ in meaning. The move made to correct what was seen as a deficiency in the old analysis utilized the same strategy as that used in the analysis of negation: a phrase structure rule was written which optionally introduced a "question morpheme," Q, and a later transformation sensitive to the presence of Q obligatorily formed the surface structure question. That is, a deep structure like 'Q it is raining' would be mapped into 'Is it raining?' Thus, it was claimed, the deep structure of a question and a declarative differ, and the hypothesis that transformations do not change meaning would be preserved. The morpheme Q had the burden of carrying whatever meaning difference exists between questions and statements. It might be mentioned that a more recent analysis suggested by J. R. Ross (1970) holds that the deep structure of 'Is it raining' would be something like 'I ask you whether it is raining or it is not raining', in which the part of the deep structure under the highest *S*, the "I ask you" is deleted by a transformation.

The Katz-Postal hypothesis serves as a constraint on transformational grammars, in the sense of "grammatical constraint" discussed above in Chapter Four. It clearly limits the class of grammars defined by the theory of universal grammar, as it postulates that arbitrary pairs of nonsynonymous sentences can never enter into transformational relations. The condition on recoverability of deletions clearly plays an important role with respect to the hypothesis that transformations do not change meaning. It will be recalled that the condition on recoverability requires that any term deleted by the operation of a transformation either be identical to a term that is not deleted on that application of that transformation, or else be one of a finite list of terms fixed for the grammar.

The condition on recoverability prevents us from deriving 'Tom ate' from 'Tom ate meat', 'Tom ate potatoes', and so on. In fact, the only source of 'Tom ate' can be 'Tom ate something', where 'something' is one of the (few) terms of English that can be freely deleted in this position. If the sentence in question could be derived from many different sources, then the deletion transformation in this case would change meaning, for 'Tom ate' is not many ways ambiguous depending on what was deleted (e.g., 'meat', 'potatoes', etc.).

6.4

Alternatives to the Standard Theory

In this section we will briefly examine a concept of linguistic structure different from the Standard Theory of *Aspects* in several fundamental ways. This theory of grammar, known as Generative Semantics, developed out of the Standard Theory historically, and remains currently under discussion. We will consider only the logical structure of this theory, without taking up the empirical data relevant to a choice among this theory, the Standard Theory, and other variants of the Standard Theory.

The converse of the Katz-Postal hypothesis that transformations preserve meaning states that if different surface structures *s* and *s'* have the same meaning, then they come from the same deep structure. (In the case of ambiguous surface structures, if *s* and *s'* have a reading in common, then some transformational sequences lead from a fixed deep structure to each, respectively.) If this converse is adopted as a research strategy—in the sense that some analysis is considered adequate only if it accomplishes the reduction of all different sentences with some particular meaning to a characteristic deep structure—then it leads quite naturally to the Universal Base Hypothesis (UBH).

The UBH states that all languages have the same deep structure, up to order of constituents. This last proviso allows for the existence of languages like Japanese, which are verb final, versus languages like Arabic, which are verb initial. The statement of grammatical relations is independent of the order of constituents.

The converse of the Katz-Postal hypothesis leads to the UBH in a number of ways. First, many of the arguments which indicate that different surface structures in English should be represented by a deep structure of a particular form seem to generalize to any language, and can be used to show that comparable surface structures have a deep structure of the same form. These arguments concern such matters as selection restrictions, scope of negation, and performatives. For example, arguments that two surface structures had a common deep structure valid for, say, Old English, would still apply to later stages of English, particularly insofar as these arguments made use of the fact that the two surface structures carried the same meaning. Clearly, even though the form of the language had changed over time, the meanings relevant to the arguments for sameness of deep structure did not (otherwise there would be a lack of translatability for at least some sentences).

These considerations that have been adduced to show that the deep structure of English has not changed (up to possible reordering of constituents) from Old to Modern English can be applied to languages even more distantly related to each other. In fact, insofar as arguments for sameness of deep structure are dependent on or a consequence of sameness of meaning, these arguments are universal. Thus it is that adopting the converse of the Katz-Postal hypothesis leads naturally to the UBH.

Under the theory that the base is universal (up to order of constituents), it follows that in learning a language the child need not learn rules of semantic interpretation to map base structures into semantic representation. That is, if the base is universal, then knowledge of deep structure is innate. Since the deep structure need not be learned by the child (other than specification of the order of constituents), he does not need language particular rules to map deep structure into meanings. If there are semantic interpretive rules at all, then under the UBH they are also universal, and thus known by the language acquirer as part of the conceptual equipment he brings to the language learning task. Notice, however, that rules of semantic interpretation would have the effect of mapping structures in one notation into structures represented in a different notation; this mapping is the same in each language. This reshuffle of notation would contribute nothing to the description of language, neither would it contribute any hypothesis concerning the nature of language. Thus, all choices of rules of semantic interpretation and universal semantic representation would be without empirical content.

The only possible state of affairs under which an interpretive semantic component would not be purely ornamental is that in which the mapping from deep structures into semantic representation is not one-one. If it is possible for a single deep structure to have different meanings, or for a number of different deep structures to have the same meaning, then an interpretive semantic component is necessary in order to represent this fact. For example, if, as has been claimed, both meanings of a sentence like 'Jones opened the door with Smith' (depending on whether Jones used Smith as an instrument, or both Jones and Smith acted as agents) come from the same syntactic deep structure, this fact would have to be represented by a component of the grammar which would be called the semantic component. Likewise, if, as has been claimed, sentences like, 'Jones saw his sister' and 'Jones saw his father's daughter' are synonymous, but come from different syntactic deep structures, then this fact (and potentially infinitely many others like it) must also be so marked by the semantic component.

The UBH, it will be recalled, developed out of accepting the converse of the Katz-Postal thesis as a working hypothesis. The Katz-Postal thesis and its converse together can be shown to rule out the possibilities either of several different deep structures having the same meaning, or of a single deep structure having two different meanings. The first possibility is ruled out because if deep structures D_1 and D_2 have the same meaning, then they correspond to surface structures with the same meaning. These must, by the converse of the Katz-Postal thesis, be derived from the same deep structure. Thus, either D_1 and D_2 have different meanings, or they are in fact not deep structures, but are derived from a common "deeper" structure. The argument leading to the conclusion that one deep structure cannot have two different meanings is slightly more complicated, but just as conclusive, given the premises. Suppose that deep structure D_1 has meanings M_1 and M_2. Now let D_1 be mapped into surface structure S_1, which also has M_1 and M_2 as possible readings. Let S_2 and S_3 be distinct surface structures which carry M_1 and M_2 as their respective meanings. Then, since S_2 and S_1 have a reading in common, they must come from the same deep structure, D_2, by the converse of the Katz-Postal thesis; S_3 and S_1 must also come from the same deep structure, D_3. If $D_2 \neq D_1$, we have two different deep structures with the same meaning, M_1, which is ruled out by the argument above. Thus it follows that $D_2 = D_1$. The same reasoning allows us to conclude that $D_3 = D_1$. Since S_2 was derived from D_1, and D_1 has two readings, then S_2 must also have two readings by the Katz-Postal thesis. In addition, S_3 must have both M_1 and M_2 as possible interpretations. We arrive at the conclusion that if a given deep structure is "ambiguous," then every surface structure derived from that deep structure has two or more readings—no surface structure can carry one and only one of the readings involved. This has in fact never been observed to happen, except, perhaps, where the ambiguity involved was a lexical ambiguity and did not involve a matter of deep structure configuration. In the case of the sentence 'Jones opened the door with

Smith' cited above, the sentences 'Jones and Smith opened the door' and 'Jones used Smith to open the door' carry the respective meanings unambiguously.

We have thus traced the line of reasoning which proceeds from accepting the converse of the Katz-Postal hypothesis in linguistic analysis. This reasoning leads to the UBH, and to the conclusion that the semantic component is ornamental and can be done away with in linguistic theory.

A further argument adduced to show the nonexistence of a semantic component in the view of grammar outlined above concerns the nature of semantic representation. It is argued that whatever the nature of this representation, it must mark, say, scope relations. For example, the meaning ambiguity in a sentence like 'All the men are not heroes' resides in whether the negation is in the scope of the universal quantifier or vice versa. Scope relations are represented by trees; whatever semantic representation may be, it at least contains enough tree structure to represent scope. But then the rules of interpretation in the alleged semantic component must map trees into trees, it is argued, and thus they look formally very much like transformational operations. Various tests seem to indicate that these rules obey all known transformational constraints, and thus are indistinguishable from transformations. The conclusion drawn from this is that the "semantic representation" is in fact the deep structure, and what might have been termed rules of semantic interpretation in an earlier theory are transformations mapping deep structures "out" to the surface, rather than mappings of deep structures "back" into semantic representation.

The view of grammar outlined above, in which there is no semantic component and deep structure is identified with the meaning of a sentence, is called Generative Semantics, the term originating in the fact that meanings are "generated" by phrase structure rules. In this theory, the boxes and arrows are redrawn as indicated below.

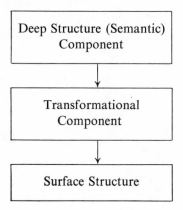

Certain attempts to account for child language acquisition within the framework of Generative Semantics have taken the following form: The base is universal up to order of constituents, and there is a fixed finite universal list of transformations (which take slightly different forms in different languages). Among this list of transformations, some are present in all languages, and some are more restricted in their occurrence. What the child must learn in acquiring his native language is (i) the order of the constituents in the base component, (ii) which of those transformations which are optionally present are in fact represented in his language, and (iii) the precise formulation of each of the transformations in his language.

In one sense, this proposal comes closer at the present time to providing an explanation of child language acquisition than does the Standard Theory, if only because the latter has failed to yield a tightly constrained class of grammars. On the other hand, the problem is solved by brute force, as it were, for the claim is that there is fundamentally only one grammar for all of human language. In other words the class of grammars from which the child must pick the grammar in his language has essentially only one member, up to the variables discussed above.

Both the Standard Theory and Generative Semantics make certain empirical predictions concerning the nature of human language. The decision between these theories, or the rejection of them both, will be based on these empirical considerations.

Bibliography

BAR-HILLEL, Y., PERLES, M., and SHAMIR, E. "On Formal Properties of Simple Phrase Structure Grammars," *Technical Report*, 4, 1960.

CARNAP, R. *Meaning and Necessity*. Chicago: University of Chicago Press, 1947.

CHOMSKY, N. Aspects of the Theory of Syntax. Cambridge: M.I.T. Press, 1965.

———. *Syntactic Structures*. The Hague: Mouton, 1957.

FREGE, G. *Begriffschrift* (1879). Trans. in Van Heijenoort, *From Frege to Gödel*. Cambridge: Harvard University Press, 1968.

KATZ, J., and POSTAL, P. *An Integrated Theory of Linguistic Description*. Cambridge: M.I.T. Press, 1964.

KIMBALL, J. "Predicates Definable over Transformational Derivations by Intersection with Regular Languages," *Information and Control*, 11, 1967.

MATES, B. *Elementary Logic*. Oxford University Press, 1965.

ROSS, J. R. "Constraints on Variables in Syntax." Unpublished Ph.D. dissertation, M.I.T., 1967.

———. "On Declarative Sentences," in Jacobs and Rosenbaum, eds., *Readings in English Transformational Grammar*. Waltham, Mass.: Ginn & Co., 1970.

TARSKI, A. "The Concept of Truth in Formalized Languages," in *Logic, Semantics, Metamathematics*. Oxford: Clarendon Press, 1935.